A Compact Guide to Balancing Your Life

Brad Lewis

NAVPRESS

Contents

THE PRACTICE OF BALANCE
Going After Balance

BALANCE IN YOUR LIFE
Seeking Balance in Your Own Life

BALANCE IN THE EVERYDAY
Living Out Balance Every Day

Acknowledgments

Thanks to my closest coworkers at NavPress—especially Paul, Don, Greg, Nanci, Melissa, and Lori—for your patience as I wrote a book while you continued with the day-to-day responsibilities we're all responsible for. Also to Glynese and Terry for their hard work once the writing was finished.

Thanks to the kind people of *Rev.* magazine at Group Publishing for their continued working relationship. I love writing for your readers, and I appreciate your willingness to let me adapt several pieces I've written for this book.

Thanks to friends and family members for responding to my e-mails to provide the Other Voices in this book. Your transparency is a powerful testimony to your faith.

Finally, above all, thanks to my wife, Esther, and my sons Nate and Trent, who didn't complain when Dad was "in his office again," and who waited patiently whenever I said, "I think I'm almost finished."

Acknowledgements

Balancing Your Life

Jesus was never in a hurry, never impressed by the numbers, never a slave of the clock. He was acting, he said, as he observed God to act—never in a hurry.

J. B. Phillips

Introduction

The baby's crying—she needs changing.

That Sunday school lesson you're supposed to teach tomorrow lies on the dining room table—unchanged from where you left it last Sunday.

Your six-year-old asks if he can finger paint but you say, "not now"—and then discover that he's already started without putting down the required three layers of newspaper.

Your spouse comes home from work late and wonders why you're not dressed for the concert you're supposed to go to tonight (and it's then that you realize neither of you called the baby-sitter).

The phone rings, the TV blares, and your head pounds. Oops, you forgot about needing to eat dinner early too. Meanwhile, the dog jumps around frantically at the back door because he needs to go out—and his barking lets you know he needs to go out *right now!*

Good grief, you think, *even the dog can't leave me alone for two minutes!*

You think of that old commercial where the harried woman slips into the bathtub and says, "Calgon, take me away!" And you realize, *Calgon ain't gonna do it today!*

If only someone else in the family would change the baby once in awhile. If only you hadn't said yes to teaching Sunday school. If only your kids would listen when you say no. If only your spouse would take a little more responsibility around the house. If only you hadn't bought that dog. If only . . . then you'd have a little balance in your life.

It seems that everyone is looking for some kind of balance in life. At the very least, people want satisfaction, contentment, or a bit of instant gratification. Yet this search for happiness or balance—whatever it is you're looking for—seems completely elusive.

Maybe it's obvious why balance eludes so many of us. According to the rather avant-garde *AdBusters* magazine, here's how the average American spends his or her day:

- Sleeping—7 hours
- Working—7.5 hours
- Commuting—1.3 hours
- Eating—1.5 hours
- Watching television—6.5 hours
- Remaining time—exactly 42 minutes for you to have to yourself[1]

Here's another way you might think about why balance is so elusive. People in metropolitan areas surveyed by McNeill Lahman/BASF Corp. said that their levels of stress, anxiety, and sadness are so high that it affects their daily life, although their symptoms weren't quite high enough to qualify as clinical depression.

Respondents listed the following stressors as their top ten:

- family concerns
- traffic
- finances
- crime
- drug violence
- work
- pollution
- personal life
- debt
- family relationships

Hmmm. It's no wonder balance seems to escape you. You're so busy that you have only forty-two minutes of free time per week. Or you're so stressed out, sad, or anxious that you may soon be on your way to a local counseling center.

So just where can you find balance? (Maybe the obvious first step is to cut back on that TV watching!) For that matter, what is balance?

Some people say that you'll find balance in your life once you take control of your circumstances. You'll read about that later, and you'll discover why trying to control your entire life may not be the best way to find a true sense of balance.

Others say that contentment and balance come from not having worries or struggles in life. Well, have you ever met anyone who doesn't have at least one worry or struggle? You'll read more about that later as well.

If you ask your friends and family, you'll quickly learn that people have a lot of ideas about how to achieve balance in life. In this book, you'll read about a number of these concepts and explore how many of them may be a part of finding balance, but none really provides the whole picture.

Focusing on the Basics

If you're looking for a bit of contentment in life, this book is meant to be a primer for you. It's just what the title says, *A Compact Guide to Balancing Your Life*, with emphasis on the "compact guide" aspect. It's chock full of ideas, concepts, tips, general thoughts, and maybe even some pop psychology, as well as some basic biblical insights about what achieving a balanced life might look like and how you might try to get there.

However, if you've been feeling completely out of sorts, if you're facing severe problems of any kind, this book simply may not be enough to help pull you out of your hole. If these words describe you, talk to a close friend who has pulled himself or herself out of the muck and mire. Or be bold enough to schedule a time to talk with your pastor. And if your doldrums seem particularly severe, don't be afraid to take that trip mentioned above to get some professional counseling.

This book isn't a substitute for any of those things. In fact, you'll read about the importance of relationships—both with others and with God—as a part of balance. So even if your feelings of imbalance or discontent aren't severe, seek out others who can help you find balance in your life.

What this book does provide, then, is a starting point. It hasn't been put together by a professional counselor or expert. Instead, it's written by someone who has found a measure of balance in his life. But even that small sense of balance is an ongoing everyday process of learning and refocusing when life gets even slightly off-kilter. And it very frequently does!

> ### Silent Destiny
>
> No trumpets sound when the important decisions of our life are made. Destiny is made known silently.
> —Agnes DeMille

A Compact Guide to Balancing Your Life is set up in an easy-to-use, reader-friendly format. You might decide to read from beginning to end, or you might want to scan the Contents and skip to the section that includes the kind of information or ideas you're looking for. The book is divided into six main categories, and each category contains a list of questions and answers. Simple as that.

Baby Steps

Remember the comedy movie, *What About Bob?* It featured Bill Murray as Bob Wiley, a completely neurotic psychological hypochondriac (say that ten times real fast). If something was a mental problem, Bob either thought he had it, or he pretended he did so that he wouldn't get it! When Bob first goes to see Dr. Leo Marvin, played by Richard Dreyfuss, Bob is an irrational basket case. He won't touch anyone or anything because of his fear of germs. He walks up dozens of floors to Dr. Marvin's office because he's afraid of elevators. The list of his neuroses goes on. Dr. Marvin, about to leave on vacation for a month, gives Bob a copy of his new book, *Baby Steps.* The book's "brilliant" premise, described by Dr. Marvin himself: overcoming your problems by breaking them down into smaller pieces, taking them one piece at a time and one day at a time.

Bob seems to catch on quickly, as he baby steps over to the window ledge, baby steps out of the office, and baby steps onto the elevator. Soon, however, baby stepping isn't quite enough, and Bob tracks down where Dr. Marvin has gone on vacation and follows him, begging not to have to wait a month before receiving further counseling. By the time Bob is done endearing himself to Dr. Marvin's family, he seems to have overcome all of his problems. He even ends up marrying Dr. Marvin's sister! However, in the meantime, Dr. Marvin becomes so irritated by Bob's persistence that he first tries to blow him up and then ends up in a mental hospital himself!

Okay, so maybe poking fun at the mental profession and people with problems isn't your thing. But problems are pretty universal, and like Bob pretending to have problems so he can't get them, if we can laugh at our imbalances, maybe they'll seem less serious.

In any event, congratulations on your desire to seek balance in life and for taking a "baby step" toward finding it by diving into this book. Pray that as you read, God will use the words of this book and Scripture to direct you to an understanding of what true balance is. And then try to put some of these ideas into practice to find a sense of balance in your own life.

The Meaning of Balance

Don't worry about the future—

worry quenches the work of grace within you. The

future belongs to God. He is in charge of all

things. Never second-guess him.

François Fénelon

Defining Balance

You might recall the hit movie *Forrest Gump*. Forrest was a bit "slow," with a limited IQ. Yet because of his innocent attitude about life, he wasn't afraid to try nearly anything. And because of his positive influence over three decades of world events, he unknowingly helped make the world a better place.

In some portions of the movie, Forrest—played by actor Tom Hanks in an Oscar-winning performance—is conversing with others sharing a bus stop bench, dispensing his mama's down-home, sage proverbs of life. His most famous line? "Mama always told me, 'Life is like a box of chocolates.' You never know what you're gonna get."

Sometimes trying to find balance in life seems like that. From day to day, "you never know what you're gonna get!"

Before you read any farther, stop for a moment to do a quick assignment. Call up a few friends and ask them what they think "living a balanced life" means. Call your mama if you want to! Go ahead—what others say could even help you more than anything you read in this book! Or at least others' answers will give you a good perspective that reflects how the people around you view life.

What did your friends say? Did you hear any advice worthy of becoming a "Gumpism"? Maybe you heard that balance means having a good attitude about life. Perhaps someone said that he thinks balance has something to do with the priorities you set. Other friends might tell you that balance is the same as simplifying your life. Another person might tell you that she tries to find balance in small ways, hoping that will help her feel okay about bigger problems in life. None of these answers is particularly wrong, but they might feel incomplete to you. Just remember, if you're trying to define balance, you'll probably get as many different answers as you have friends.

Other Voices

Some people understand balance to mean that life is neatly and evenly divided between the various components of our days—family, work, friends, recreation, and so on. But for me, balance is less a matter of portioning out my time and attentions, and more a matter of having a place to stand that lets me weigh the importance of demands and events, distinguishing the critical from the merely urgent, and touching base regularly with the things that matter.

—Tim

What about you? Stop reading again for a minute and either mentally or with pen and paper list some words that make you think of balance in life. What words would you use to create a definition of balance? Does contentment mean the same as balance? Does satisfaction about where you are in life mean the same thing as balance? Is being authentic a part of being balanced? What about terms such as "perfection" or "harmony with others"?

As you begin or continue a search for balance in your life, it might help to think about some terms that seem to mean the same thing as balance but perhaps really mean something else. Or maybe some of these concepts only reflect a part of what balance is all about.

Take a look at some of these terms and explore what they mean, how they probably present an incomplete idea of balance, and how you can still use these concepts as you try to find balance in your life.

And if you ever find yourself on a park bench, don't be afraid to tell a stranger what you've learned about balance.

Some people I know seem almost perfect — is perfection another word for balance?

One way you can think about perfection is to think of something being without fault or defect. Of course, your own common sense tells you that perfection is something that you simply can't achieve. That doesn't mean that a lot of people don't try to reach some level of perfection.

> God desires that you strive for holiness even if it's simply unattainable apart from His intimate intervention in your life.

It's fairly common, for example, for first-time parents to say that they want to be perfect. They'll visit stores for the latest and greatest books on babies and child rearing. They'll place subscriptions for several parenting magazines in order to read everything they can get their hands on about hands-on baby care. With first babies, parents will grind their own baby food and use only cloth diapers from a diaper service because they've read that those are the best ways to care for their baby (or they'll use only disposable diapers because it's better against baby's skin than those harsh detergents needed to get cloth diapers sanitary). Whatever. But it doesn't take long for most parents to realize that they will and do make mistakes in their parenting. And perfect parenting eludes them.

And, of course, there are times when you hope that others are perfect. For example, if you're having laser surgery to correct your vision or bypass surgery on your heart to take care of a blockage, you hope that your surgeon is perfect. But there's a reason doctors carry malpractice insurance and a reason that patients sign waivers before they undergo those procedures. No one is perfect.

The same is true of trying to live a balanced life. No matter how you measure balance—whether by some rule of perfection or even some lower standard—it's simply unachievable on your own. You can try to be balanced. You can study balance. You can make every effort to be balanced in every area of life. But because you're not perfect, you can't maintain that balance for very long. True balance, as you'll read later, can only come from a personal relationship with God through His Son, Jesus Christ.

Jesus even used the word "perfect" in what sounds like a command. In Matthew 5:48, He said, "Be perfect, therefore, as your heavenly Father is perfect." So Jesus must want you to strive for perfection, right? Maybe the thinking above is simply incorrect.

Not so fast! Is it possible that Jesus was simply holding up for us the standard that God expects, even if He knows that we're unable to reach that standard? In fact, some Bible scholars say that rather than perfect here, Jesus really exhorts you to "be mature." God desires that you strive for holiness even if it's simply unattainable apart from His intimate intervention in your life.

The way Eugene Peterson translates this passage in *The Message* might help you better grasp the idea of the way Christ wants you to live: "What I'm saying is, *Grow up*. You're kingdom subjects. Now live like it. Live out your God-created identity. Live generously and graciously toward others, the way God lives toward you."

Another funny thing about trying to be perfect is that some people who try to achieve perfection have a hard time getting anything done or making any decisions at all. Maybe you'd like to make the perfect decision about buying a new car. You want to get the best price, the best deal, the best financing, and/or the best lease rates and terms. You spend hours and days researching about the best new car for you and your family. You search the Internet for information on how to make the best deals with

---

Risk Taking

We cannot escape fear. We can only transform it into a companion that accompanies us on all our exciting adventures. . . . Take a risk a day—one small or bold stroke that will make you feel great once you have done it.

—Susan Jeffers

salespeople, the current interest rates, the very best lease terms. You actually go to automobile dealerships and test drive your top five picks for cars. Finally, three weeks later, you make a decision. You head off to the dealership to make your deal, armed with all your information. You're going to end up with one of the best values on the road, and you're not going to be taken by some slick car salesperson. But when you get there—three weeks after you started this whole process—you find out that the price of the car you want has gone up, two new recalls for that model were issued just this morning, interest rates on auto financing have risen

Other Voices

If I compare myself to someone who seems to have it all together, then it's hard to feel good about myself. But if I remember to see myself as God sees me—with love and forgiveness for my failures—I get my sense of balance back.

—Lisa

half a percent, and—to top it off—the dealer doesn't even have the color you wanted. What just happened? You were your own victim of "analysis paralysis." In your search for making the perfect car deal, you so thoroughly researched and analyzed your buying decision that you missed the window of opportunity to get your dream car.

Whether you're susceptible to analysis paralysis or you strive for perfection for some other reason, remember that perfection is simply unattainable for humans. Instead of trying to achieve perfection, think about striving for excellence in all that you do as part of seeking balance in your life. Excellence means trying your hardest, doing your best, making the right choice rather than the easy choice. We can try and try, but as sinful beings, perfection is an unattainable goal. (See also **How does a sinul nature—a fallen world—prevent me from having a sense of balance in my life?** on page 80.)

The apostle Paul wrote to his young protégé, Timothy, that God expected his best. Paul's words hold true for you as well: "Do your best to present yourself to God as one approved, a workman who does not need to be ashamed and who correctly handles the word of truth" (2 Timothy 2:15). God doesn't expect your perfection. He expects your best for Him.

Summary

- Perfection is elusive; no one on earth is perfect.
- Balance as a whole is similar to the idea of perfection—it's also elusive. Yet balance is a more desirable goal than perfection.
- Christ calls you to be perfect, even though that's unattainable in your earthly body; but He still desires for you to be holy and mature in your faith.
- Beware of analysis paralysis.
- Instead of perfection, pursue excellence as part of seeking balance.
- God doesn't expect perfection; He expects your best.

Is balanced living the same as feeling satisfied?

Being completely satisfied is nearly as elusive as perfection. Satisfaction is a feeling of being fulfilled or pleased, so it does have a role to play in feeling balanced. But again, it's a feeling that is fleeting.

Satisfaction can be positive or negative. People who smoke sometimes crave nicotine so much that they say they "feel satisfied" when they can light up and get that chemical into their system. Before they were banned from television, cigarette commercials played on this by showing green meadows and running streams or some other vision of a "good life" that resulted from smoking.

The same feeling of satisfaction is true of people who crave alcohol or prescription painkillers or illegal drugs. Their bodies crave an addictive element in these substances, and they only feel satisfied when they get that chemical into their systems. In a similar way, some people who shoplift say they get a "high" by succeeding. All of these illustrate a kind of satisfaction, but they're probably not good things.

If you can't relate to any of these examples, think instead about eating a huge meal. Maybe remember last Thanksgiving. You smell the turkey, sweet potatoes, fresh-baked rolls, pumpkin pies, and the rest of the meal cooking at various times during the day. A beautiful table is set using the best china, crystal, and silver. Finally, the big moment to begin the meal arrives. As the turkey is carved, even more of that wonderful aroma is released into the room. And when you finally get to eat, you load your plate full once, twice, even three times. Your stomach is so full that you can barely move. But a smile creeps across your face because you can't remember the last time you ate so much and your hunger was so satisfied.

But by the next day at the very latest, that feeling of satisfaction is gone. Over the next few days you eat turkey sandwiches, turkey soup, turkey casseroles, turkey and eggs for breakfast. Each meal you fill up on the same tired leftovers of sweet potatoes, mashed potatoes, and cranberry sauce. These once-wonderful foods begin to all taste the same—like the inside of your refrigerator! And with each bite you find less and less satisfaction with filling up on turkey and related Thanksgiving leftovers.

Satisfaction is like that—feeling satisfied is something you want right now, immediate gratification. But the immediacy is also what makes it a fleeting sensation. So rather than seeking satisfaction as part of balancing your life, perhaps you'd be better served trying for a more long-term feeling. In fact, you may want to ask yourself these questions: Will this action that gives me a satisfied feeling truly provide an overall sense of contentment and balance? Or will the action—like a huge Thanksgiving dinner—merely offer a temporary sensation of satisfaction?

Other Voices

True satisfaction comes only when we let God have complete control and trust Him for the outcome, even though we may feel "unbalanced" by what God requires of us. The important thing is who defines balance for you. If you define it for yourself and try to live within those parameters, you're taking control of your life away from God. If God defines your balance and you live according to His purpose for your life, your life will be balanced by God, not yourself.

—Lisa

Summary

- Satisfaction is something you can achieve for a short time.
- However, it's a fleeting feeling; satisfaction tends to be more of an immediate gratification.
- Satisfaction isn't always a good thing (for example, drug abuse can bring a short-term feeling of satisfaction, but the long-term effects are completely unsatisfactory).
- Satisfaction isn't necessarily bad either. To gauge whether something will bring a sense of true balance rather than a fleeting feeling, ask, "Will this feeling last longer than a few hours?"

Does balance mean feeling in harmony with the world around me?

One of the meanings of harmony is a sense of calm. This isn't necessarily some New Age-type concept. In fact, the Bible lists many verses about having an inner peace (see Isaiah 26:3; John 16:33; Romans 5:1; Philippians 4:7; Hebrews 12:11; 13:20). Ironically, as with many of the concepts related to feeling a sense of balance in life, you have to battle your natural tendency with the idea of seeking inner peace or harmony.

Another way to think of harmony is complementing those around you. You might desire to "fit in" in an appropriate way. As with many of these qualities, part of feeling a sense of balance may include times of feeling in harmony with the world around you. But you'll have many times when you won't feel connected to the outer world at all.

A simple example: Maybe you've been with friends or extended family watching a video that you mutually decided to rent. But by the middle of the movie, you feel completely uncomfortable. Maybe it's explicit scenes of sex or violence. Perhaps it's the characters' use of profanity. Maybe it's lewd humor. Or perhaps it's a gruesome or twisting story line that simply makes you feel like you shouldn't be watching this movie. As the others laugh or otherwise seem to enjoy the movie, you find yourself writhing in your seat, wishing you could escape. For the moment, you feel completely disconnected— and totally out of harmony—with people you may care for, love, and respect.

Some people try to meditate their way into a sense of inner peace. Others escape from as much of the world as they can, figuring that they can find peace without the external distractions of the world.

Some people try to meditate their way into a sense of inner peace. Others escape from as much of the world as they can.

In fact, you might remember Howard Hughes. He was born into great wealth and during his lifetime was one of America's most famous people. In addition to his wealth, he possessed a keen intellect and enjoyed great achievements during the height of his lifetime, including producing some forty motion pictures and designing and flying airplanes. You might guess that with such wealth and success, he'd have found happiness to match his fortune. But in the later years of his life, Hughes became a complete recluse. He suffered from obsessive-compulsive disorder, a mental illness that can cause ritualistic behavior and unusual habits. Hughes, for example, became obsessed with germs and cleanliness. During the last fifteen to twenty years of his life, Hughes occupied himself by purchasing casinos, hotels, and land in and around Las Vegas, Nevada. He moved constantly to remain a recluse and to ensure his privacy. He worked for days without sleep or food, and became increasingly deranged from excessive drug use. He finally died of kidney failure in 1976.[1]

The point of Hughes' story is to warn against thinking that you can escape to some mountain cabin or secluded monastery in an attempt to find peace and harmony. The

Near the Light

Truly, it is in the darkness
that one finds the light, so
when we are in sorrow,
then this light is nearest of
all to us.

—Meister Eckhart

same is true of escaping inside yourself even if you physically stay connected with the world. While connection with others doesn't assure a sense of balance, disconnecting from others certainly doesn't seem to guarantee that you'll find peace. Instead, you'll likely find loneliness, paranoia, and maybe you'll even succumb to some sort of mental imbalance.

On the other hand, Scripture calls you to push against your human nature and instead surrender yourself so that the peace of Christ can fill you through the power of the Holy Spirit. Jesus said, "The Counselor, the Holy Spirit, whom the Father will send in my name, will teach you all things and will remind you of everything I have said to you. Peace I leave with you; my peace I give you" (John 14:26-27). Even this doesn't mean that your life will be without troubles, suffering, or struggles. In fact, Scripture essentially promises that these qualities that you might think of as negative will always be a part of life this side of heaven. But troubles, suffering, and struggles do have a purpose. (For more on suffering, see **According to Scripture, why do suffering and struggle have to be a part of balancing life?** on page 61, and **How does my response to suffering and struggling affect my sense of balance?** on page 86.)

Like many other pieces of the puzzle of living a balanced life, seeking harmony with the world around you, while it sounds good, is yet another elusive quality. There's simply a lot about the world—whether it's your home, workplace, community, or beyond—that you can't control. That places a lot of pressure on you to try to "harmonize" with the cacophony of noises the external world is making. And as soon as you feel in tune with one influence or relationship, you'll likely be out of tune with another.

Instead of trying to feel in harmony with the world, you might want to aim for the internal feeling of peacefulness that Scripture promises. This will give you peace no matter what's going on externally. Again, that inner peace comes not from trying to "will" peace or harmony to exist inside you. Rather, true inner peace comes from surrendering your life to Jesus and allowing the Holy Spirit to fill you with peace that can come only from God. Even Jesus relied on God completely—in fact, because of who He was, it was impossible for Jesus to act except in dependence on the Father.[2] John 5:19 says, "I tell you the truth, the Son can do nothing by himself; he can do only what he sees his Father doing, because whatever the Father does the Son also does."

Summary

- Feeling in harmony with what goes on around you is having an internal sense of calm in spite of what is occurring.
- True inner peace can't be found through meditation, withdrawal, or any external means.
- Neither can inner peace come from simply trying to "fit in" with the world around you.
- Too many things going on around you are out of your control.
- Inner peace and harmony can only come from a relationship with Christ.

Some people say balance comes in the small things — is that true?

Several years ago, Richard Carlson wrote a best-selling book titled *Don't Sweat the Small Stuff*. Generally, he emphasized that life is made up mostly of very small events that don't really merit the importance we place on them. He then gives a hundred prescriptives to ensure that you will not ever emit a single drop of sweat. A lot of it is valuable advice.

In the introduction of this book, Carlson says that his thoughts and writings are based on Zen philosophy. So, of course it would be wise to compare these thoughts

The Last Detail

"What's the price of a pet canary? Some loose change, right? And God cares what happens to it even more than you do. He pays even greater attention to you, down to the last detail—even numbering the hairs on your head!

—Matthew 10:29-30, MSG

with what Scripture has to say. Then, it matters far less about where the ideas come from and more if they're true or not. If they're the truth, they belong to God, because He is Truth. (In other words, if something is true, don't be afraid to claim it, because no matter what individual or group tries to claim it, truth always belongs to God.)

So what does the Bible have to say about "the small stuff"? Consider Matthew 10:29-31: "Are not two sparrows sold for a penny? Yet not one of them will fall to the ground apart from the will of your Father. And even the very hairs of your head are all numbered. So don't be afraid; you are worth more than many sparrows." Also Matthew 6:25-30: "Do not worry about your life, what you will eat or drink; or about your body, what you will wear. . . . Look at the birds of the air; they do not sow or reap or store away in barns, and yet your heavenly Father feeds them. Are you not much more valuable than they? Who of you by worrying can add a single hour to his life? And why do you worry about clothes? See how the lilies of the field grow. They do not labor or spin. Yet I tell you that not even Solomon in all his splendor was dressed like one of these. If that is how God clothes the grass of the field, which is here today and tomorrow is thrown into the fire, will he not much more clothe you?"

So, what's the difference between what Scripture says and what the world says? When the culture says "Don't sweat the small stuff," it's trying to get you to look for balance from some source other than God. But Scripture clearly points you toward God when it admonishes you not to worry, not to toil, not to "sweat." The world is telling you to look for and take the easy path. But Scripture often points out that the world's idea of how to approach life is the opposite of God's plan: "But [the Lord] said to me, 'My grace is sufficient for you, for my power is made perfect in weakness.' . . . That is why, for Christ's sake, I delight in weaknesses, in insults, in hardships, in persecutions, in difficulties. For when I am weak, then I am strong" (2 Corinthians 12:9-10).

Another question you need to ask yourself is whether the small stuff will really bring balance to your life. Will finding balance in the little things make the big things disappear? If you clean your desk or your house, or lose those last ten pounds, or organize your photo albums, will your life suddenly feel in balance? Well, sure, these things might help, especially if one of them is really weighing on you. But the truth is that taking care of these small things will probably

> ## Sleep in Peace
>
> Have courage for the great sorrows of life, and patience for the small ones. And when you have laboriously accomplished your daily task, go to sleep in peace. God is awake.
>
> —Victor Hugo

bring only a temporary measure of feeling good about yourself. You might feel good for a few hours about what you've accomplished, but it probably won't make your whole life feel balanced.

Perhaps the best advice Carlson gives is remembering what is "small stuff." Imbalance can come when you exaggerate and magnify the little things and suddenly they become big things. Whether or not you sweat the small stuff might be a matter of semantics. What's small to someone else might loom large for you. But Scripture still encourages you not to waste your time or effort worrying about those things. Like many aspects of seeking balance, not worrying comes from surrendering those worries to God and leaving them with Him.

Is a balanced life the same as being fulfilled?

Fulfillment could be defined as filling up or making full. But when you define a word with part of itself, it's not very helpful, is it? So let's do better. Fulfillment can be a synonym for satisfaction. So you might want to also read the section that answers the question, **Is balanced living the same as feeling satisfied?** on page 26.

Fulfillment can also be thought of as developing your full potential. Certainly the Bible speaks of that concept, but perhaps in a different way than society thinks of it. Scripture points to that full potential as having its source in God. The apostle Paul

A Jesus-Honoring Life

We pray for you all the time—pray that our God will make you fit for what he's called you to be, pray that he'll fill your good ideas and acts of faith with his own energy so that it all amounts to something. If your life honors the name of Jesus, he will honor you.
—2 Thessalonians 1:11-12, MSG

wrote this about fulfillment: "We constantly pray for you, that our God may count you worthy of his calling, and that by his power he may fulfill every good purpose of yours and every act prompted by your faith" (2 Thessalonians 1:11). Paul was saying that for Christians, fulfillment comes because both purposes and actions should have their source in God. And because of that, both your motives and your deeds will be accomplished by God's power.

On the other hand, the culture you live in often seems to think of fulfillment—even the idea of living up to your full potential—as being equivalent with filling up your life. The problem with this view of fulfillment is that it can be difficult to know when to stop filling. Unlike with a water glass, which you can tell when it's almost full and therefore turn off the tap, filling up your life is more of a blind task. In other words, many people are tempted to keep filling and filling and filling until nothing else fits. In fact, some people fill to overflowing. Then, when a crisis or emergency comes along, they have no capacity left to take it on.

Here's one example: Not too many years ago, a lot was written about women in the workplace. A debate raged about whether women should work outside the home, if they had to financially or if they were choosing to, and if it was all fair to their families and children. Many women responded that they could do it all—have a career, children, home, spouse, and everything else. They declared that it was their right to fill up their lives in all of these ways.

The debate raged on for years, and it even continues in some circles. The debate isn't important in this discussion. What is important is what society learned during this time. That is, fulfillment isn't the same as filling up life. You can stack up all kinds of roles in life: spouse, parent, boss, employee, elder at church, president of the PTA. Or you can fill up your days with tasks: Get up, get the kids ready for school, make school lunches, take the kids to school, get to work by nine, meet clients, make phone calls, answer e-mails, do a power lunch, consume massive quantities of caffeine and sugar to make it through the afternoon, call the kids to make sure they're doing homework, clean the desk and file paperwork to be ready for the next workday, pick up dry cleaning on the way home, get stuck in traffic, use the cell phone to call home to say that you're stuck in traffic, stop at the grocery store for easy-to-make dinner, prepare easy-to-make dinner, battle to get everyone around the same table for dinner, run out the door for a committee meeting at church, rush home to get the kids into bed, collapse into bed at least an hour later than planned, set the alarm and look forward to doing it all again the next day! And you know what—this isn't even a complete list for a lot of people!

Well, anyway, this all sounds very fulfilling, doesn't it? Not really. It becomes obvious rather quickly that this filling up of life doesn't equal fulfillment. And this is just an example. Men and women seem equally likely to fill up their lives in similar ways.

The point is that many people have learned that fulfillment comes much less from their career or other responsibilities in life, and instead—as noted earlier—can only come from a relationship with God. In fact, when you line up the mission or goals that you have in life with what God desires for you, and take action to fulfill that God-given purpose, you'll feel a sense of balance. It's then that He will be fulfilling your life.

In Paul's other letter to the church in Thessalonica, he wrote these words that seem to emphasize how only those actions and deeds that originate with and emanate from God will be fulfilling: "We continually remember before our God and Father your work produced by faith, your labor prompted by love, and your endurance inspired by hope in our Lord Jesus Christ" (1 Thessalonians 1:3).

Isn't balance at least partly just your attitude or perspective of things?

These are good thoughts. Attitude and perspective. Let's look at them one at a time.

Attitude is a feeling or emotion about something. An attitude in itself can be good or bad. Your job is a good example of this. You might have a job that you

Other Voices

Balance is one of those fat-bottomed clowns I used to punch as a kid. It always manages to right itself, no matter how hard it gets hit.
— Tim

completely love, one where you can't wait to get up in the morning and get to work because you just adore everything about it. Your boss is so considerate, the people you work with are fun and fulfilled in what they do, you own the tasks you've been given and they have great significance, and the money you get paid for doing it is more than you ever hoped to make. It's easy to have a good attitude about this kind of job, isn't it?

But maybe you have a job you totally hate, one where on Monday morning you start counting the minutes until Friday afternoon. You abhor everything about what you do — your boss seems to be shady, the people you work with are all trying to get out, you have menial and meaningless tasks to do, and best of all, your pay completely stinks. Like the pay, it's pretty easy to have a stinky attitude about this kind of job.

Because your attitude is based on feelings or emotions, it's probably not a good measure of balance. Your emotions aren't all bad — in fact, they can be a good barometer to detect if you're feeling unbalanced in some way. But because emotions depend on so many external things that you can't control, they're not a complete or accurate measure of balance.

So don't measure balance in your life by your attitude. You'll be shortchanging yourself, because your life is so much more.

The idea of perspective is a little more complete than attitude. Perspective means to view things in their true relationship to each other. So when you try to gain perspective about something, you can take into account your attitude, but you'll also measure that emotion and others against the other aspects of your life, such as your physical condition, your mental development, and your spiritual health.

Go back to that good attitude about your job. If you bring some perspective to that situation, you may realize that while you're essentially happy for the time being, this isn't what you feel God called you to do with your life. Or maybe the work is meaningful, but it hasn't changed for five years. Because you can look beyond the emotion of the moment, perspective allows you to get a bigger view of your life.

The same is true of the job you have a bad attitude about. If you add perspective, you might be able to see that maybe your boss isn't shady, he just has all kinds of responsibility with no authority or budget to accomplish what he's supposed to. Perspective might allow you to see that while you loathe what you're doing, you can stick it out a few more months to see if that promotion might come through or if your transfer to another department and a more fulfilling position materializes.

However, perspective still isn't a complete way to think about balance. If attitude is mostly an emotional thing, then your own perspective about a situation might be too logical or calculated to measure balance. Perspective might be an objective evaluation tool for you to use to gauge whether or not you're living a balanced life, but perspective alone can't make you feel balance in life.

Does authenticity have something to do with balance?

Authentic basically means being trustworthy and believable. Deeper than simply telling the truth (although that's a part of it), being authentic is more of an ongoing reputation that you gain rather than a single event of being truthful. Because your lifestyle is one of being trustworthy and honest, authenticity allows you to live with much less stress in your life. And times of stress can easily knock your life off balance.

So, authenticity can help you with balance in life. For example, maybe you recall making up some excuse in high school about why you didn't get your homework done. You told your teacher that false reason—maybe that you had to help your parents work on the house or your dad made you mow the lawn or that Grandma died. But, of course, you couldn't tell your parents these same excuses because they knew that they hadn't worked on repairs around the house for three years, that your dad always mowed the lawn himself, and that Grandma was sipping iced tea in her retirement condo down in Miami. So you had to tell Mom and Dad a different fib: The assignment isn't due for two more weeks; the teacher has been out sick for three weeks and it's not due until she's back; or water pipes broke and the school building flooded, but it wasn't on the news because they don't want parents to panic.

Because your lifestyle is one of being trustworthy and honest, authenticity allows you to live with much less stress in your life.

Okay, this might be worse than any white lie you've ever told. But maybe it at least dredges up memories of the stress and panic you felt when you had to remember which little story you told to whom. One little set of lies doesn't necessarily make you inauthentic. But if this kind of behavior becomes a pattern for you, it could mean that you need to check whether or not you're an authentic person.

Authenticity is also about being real. It means that who you are on the inside is reflected in the things you do and say on the outside. It means not being "two-faced"—thinking and feeling one way internally, but showing a different external face to those around you

Relational psychologist Neil Clark Warren did a good job of linking the idea of contentment with authenticity in his book *Finding Contentment*. He lists ten characteristics of authentic people. Note how many of these have to do as much with an internal authenticity as they do with relationships with others.

1. Authentic people live in the present.
2. Authentic people are free from fear.
3. Authentic people are not judgmental.
4. Authentic people genuinely appreciate themselves.
5. Authentic people hunger for the truth.
6. Authentic people are adaptable and flexible.
7. Authentic people have a strong sense of gratitude.
8. Authentic people love to laugh and are lighthearted.
9. Authentic people exhibit a high degree of dignity.
10. Authentic people sleep well.[3]

Authenticity may be another barometer of balance in your life. Being authentic means that you have nothing to hide—again, because what's inside you is what the people around you see on the outside. Like most people, if you're so truthful with yourself and others that you're not afraid to let people see the real you, you're pretty likely to have a sense of internal peace. Your transparency—having nothing to hide—shows that your own life is pretty balanced.

Use Warren's list on the previous page to test yourself. Does each statement describe you? If so, look for ways to maintain that level of authenticity in your life. If some statements don't match up with who you are, explore ways to put into your life the things that you want to radiate from your life authentically.

Good or Blight?

How do you suppose what you say is worth anything when you are so foul-minded? It's your heart, not the dictionary, that gives meaning to your words. A good person produces good deeds and words season after season. An evil person is a blight on the orchard.

—Matthew 12:34-35, MSG

What about gratitude and thankfulness ... don't they have something to do with living a balanced life?

In a quick word, yes. See number seven in Dr. Warren's list.

However, like many of the other concepts discussed in this section, the idea of being thankful for your lot in life is just a part of balance, not the complete picture. So how does it fit in?

The definition of gratitude is pretty simple, because it means the attitude of being grateful or thankful. So to expand on that, think about some of the synonyms for gratitude (keeping in mind that because these words are all similar in meaning, they all use each other as definitions). But consider the subtle variations in their meanings.

Gratefulness — Deeply appreciative of kindness or benefits you've received. Note that the idea of gratefulness is being thankful for good things, gifts you've received, decisions or actions that have benefited you. Gratefulness by definition somewhat omits the idea of being thankful for negative things in life.

Thankfulness — A gratefulness or expression of appreciation for a kindness or favor. Again, being thankful doesn't necessarily include expressing gratitude for areas of life you dislike. But you might tend to think of thankfulness as that automatic response that you give or receive for even the most simple acts of kindness, such as holding open the door for the person walking behind you, or when a fellow diner passes the salt or butter. Because many expressions of thanks fall into this automatic category, it's also easy to not put much weight behind the words used to express the thanks. In fact, the words often don't consist of much more than "thank you," because the act that prompted the thanks has just occurred. This makes it unnecessary to say, "Thanks for holding open the door." But it also renders the thankfulness nearly meaningless, or at most, trivial.

Recognition — This word has other meanings, but it can be used along with the idea of gratefulness. In that respect, it means the acknowledgment of an achievement, service, or merit. You might think of receiving an employee-of-the-month award at work or how a military officer receives a medal for meritorious service. Even pay increases are often tied to merit, a recognition of the good work you've done in the past year. Still, like the other terms used to describe gratitude, recognition tends to be tied up with positive thoughts. However, it at least tends to have some weighty meaning; the expression of recognition usually needs to be expressed along with what specifically is being recognized.

Appreciation — One of the meanings of appreciation is expressing gratitude or thankful recognition. For example, if someone retires after thirty years of service at a single company, the owners might express their appreciation by presenting the retiree with a gold watch. Again, it's not common to think of expressing appreciation for negative situations in life. An employee who leaves after just six months of work is unlikely to receive a farewell party—perhaps that employee doesn't even merit lunch with the people in his department or donuts during the morning coffee break. He's never established relationships with his coworkers nor demonstrated loyalty to the company. In other words, with appreciation, there needs to be an act to appreciate before you can easily demonstrate this kind of recognition.

Acknowledgment—This word is slightly different from some of the others listed here. It leans a bit outside the idea of thankfulness, and tilts a little more toward simple statement of fact. In addition to expressing appreciation of something, you might think of acknowledgment as the idea of simply recognizing that something is true. For example, a receipt that you receive when you make a purchase is an acknowledgment. It's a proof that you might retain in case you need to return the merchandise or, if it's later found to be defective, to demonstrate that indeed you purchased it at a particular store. In these cases, except for the cursory "thank you" you receive at the time of purchase and the "thank you for doing business with us" printed on the bottom of the receipt, there isn't necessarily any gratefulness or gratitude expressed.

Well, these definitions demonstrate that it's relatively easy to think about being grateful for the things you like about life. But as the different definitions also demonstrate, it's almost unnatural to think about being thankful for the parts of life that you don't care for or that just plain stink.

Like many other areas of seeking balance, Scripture has a slightly different message than the

> ### Gratitude
>
> The most important prayer in the world is just two words long: "Thank you."
>
> —Meister Eckhart

world does when it comes to the idea of gratitude. Beginning with Judaic customs and laws in the Old Testament, God has commanded His followers to show their thanks to Him. This is never tied to good or bad times. Instead, it's related to God's general and overall goodness and justice and mercy. The laws of feasts and festivals in the Old Testament, for example, are calendar events that aren't necessarily tied to prosperous times (such as Exodus 23:14-19). These festivals were much more about expressing thankfulness to God for who He is and what He's already done with His overall plan.

The New Testament echoes this idea. Ephesians 5:19-20, in the context of the apostle Paul giving pretty simple and clear instructions about how to live as followers of Christ every day, says, "Sing and make music in your heart to the Lord, always giving thanks to God the Father for everything, in the name of our Lord Jesus Christ." *Always* is a key word here; you're not given any grace periods where you are given time off from expressing thanks to God. *Everything* is also a key word; you can't exclude anything that you don't feel thankful for. Paul is stating that God has put or allowed everything you experience into your life for a reason, and you're to be thankful for it and for God's care for you.

What if you've been diagnosed with cancer? What if you have an abusive spouse? What if you have to declare bankruptcy? What if you've lost a baby? Do you need to be thankful for these situations? And what about day-to-day disappointments—having a bad day at work, struggling to make ends meet financially, getting stuck in traffic on your daily commute? Do you have to give God thanks for these? Apparently. Or at least you need to be thankful for God's love and care for you during those times—and acknowledge that these unfortunate situations at the very least allow God to draw you closer to Himself in ways that might not have been possible without the experience. Imagine the sense of balance and peacefulness you'll feel if you can be thankful *always* and for *everything*.

You might lie awake at night with fear about your health issues, so perhaps you can't even fathom the thought of actually giving God thanks for a potentially deadly illness. Yet one Christian patient, whose cancer went into remission for the requisite number of years until she was declared cancer-free, actually lamented briefly about being cured and healed of her cancer. Of course, she said that she was thankful for freedom from treatments and tests. But she added that her illness drew her so much closer to God than she'd ever felt before that she was slightly afraid that her clean bill of health would mean never feeling that way again.

Give yourself a challenge: Any time you feel like grumbling or complaining about something, stop and tell God that you don't always understand why things happen, but you're thankful He's working in your life.

Summary

- Gratitude is the attitude of being grateful or thankful.
- Gratitude and similar words tend to focus on the idea of thankfulness for the positive events of life—the kindness or favor of others.
- Often, the idea of thankfulness minimizes being grateful for everything life throws your way, especially the negative aspects such as illnesses, struggles, crises, and so on.
- Scripture calls us to thank God for who He is, as well as His love and care for us, rather than individual blessings He heaps on us.
- The Bible calls us to be thankful to God always and for everything, not just the favors and kindnesses we receive from God.
- Balance comes when we're drawn closer to God by being thankful through and in spite of our circumstances in life.

Is balance the same as contentment?

Some of the synonyms for contentment are happiness, satisfaction, pleasure, gratification, comfort, and peace. Like the word contentment itself, these words all seem as though they belong in your vocabulary if you have a feeling of balance in life.

But another meaning of contentment includes the idea of limiting yourself—in terms of what you require of yourself and others, of what you desire for yourself and others, and the actions you take to pursue your requirements and desires.

In many ways, the pursuit of this kind of contentment is closely related to balance. Certainly, defining contentment this way is close to the heart of how Scripture speaks of contentment—in essence, denying yourself so that God can instill a sense of balance within you. Scripture often refers to internal peace that's available if you give yourself completely to God and His will for your life. As you read earlier, Jesus said, "Peace I leave with you; my peace I give you. I do not give to you as the world gives. Do not let your hearts be troubled and do not be afraid" (John 14:27).

Contentment, peace, balance—they're really not about taking all of the things that have stacked up in your life and trying to organize and prioritize them.

When Jesus encouraged—actually commanded—you not to be troubled or afraid, He was talking about surrendering your cares and worries to God. His words are complemented by the apostle Paul's familiar words in Philippians 4: "Do not be anxious about anything, but in everything, by prayer and petition, with thanksgiving, present your requests to God. And the peace of God, which transcends all understanding, will guard your hearts and your minds in Christ Jesus" (verses 6-7).

So contentment, peace, balance—they're really not about taking all of the things that have stacked up in your life and trying to organize and prioritize them. While that sometimes may be an appropriate way to find a measure of balance—especially in the daily sense—a true and ongoing sense of balance is often the opposite of how we might think of it. Rather than trying to take everything in life and stacking it all up neatly as high as you can figuratively reach, balance is also about limiting the number of things in your life that you're trying to stack up. It's about throwing out of your life the stresses and pressures and illogical responsibilities that make you feel out of balance—in fact, surrendering those to God—and *then* asking God to help you prioritize and reorganize what's left.

Enjoy the Journey

Slow down and enjoy life. It's not only the scenery you miss by going too fast—you also miss the sense of where you are going and why.
— Eddie Cantor

What's so important about relinquishing or eliminating the worrisome things in life? Unless you're a hermit or some other form of recluse, life is already filled with enough stressors and pressures. Maybe you have to deal with stop-and-go traffic on your commute to and from work. Perhaps your child has a learning disability. Maybe your spouse places unreasonable demands on your time. Or perhaps your stress is as simple as having ten minutes to buy a few things at the grocery store, but the one checkout line open takes fifteen minutes to get through. The point is, life itself brings stress.

So if you can eliminate other things that knock your life out of balance by simply surrendering them to God, you'll be better prepared for the pressures you still have to deal with—with His help, too, of course.

> ### Uncharacteristic Behavior
>
> If you are under stress and your life is out of balance, get all dressed up and go to McDonald's. Enjoy looking like an idiot. Make people smile. Act like nothing is wrong with your attire. Smile back at the people staring at you. Enjoy life! Do something uncharacteristic of your usual personality. Unwind.[4]

So, get to the point already — what is balance?

Well, a number of these questions have already included a lot about the meaning of the word "balance." But let's try to dig a little deeper here.

Take a good look at the page you're reading. Notice the white space around the edges. Remember the term for that? Margins. You might remember the idea of "setting margins" from your high school typing class. Even when the business world had progressed to—gasp—the electric typewriter, you still had to reach above the return carriage of the machine and use two sliding mechanisms to lock in the margins.

In these days of electronic word processing programs, you typically don't have to set margins any more. When you start up a word-processing program such as Microsoft Word or WordPerfect, a standard or templated document opens and default margins are already set for you. Most of the time, whether you're typing a letter, a memo for work, or writing a term paper or book, these margins work just fine.

Unfortunately, life isn't quite the same. You don't wake up each new day with templated margins already set for you. You need to revert to the old method—like in the days of typewriters—and set your margins manually.

Dr. Richard Swenson wrote a best-selling book, *Margin*, a few years ago. In it he contrasted the idea of an overloaded life with a life that leaves margin, particularly for the unexpected junk that comes at you simply because you're a human being. Look at the list he created which catalogs many areas of life that you need to seek balance between. Don't look too long, because when you dissect your life in this way, the whole goal of seeking balance can seem unreasonable or even impossible. Instead, read the list and tuck it away in the recesses of your mind as you continue reading about ways to find balance in life.

Work	Leisure	Assertiveness	Submissiveness
Action	Meditation	Structure	Spontaneity
Leading	Following	Confidence	Humility
Speaking	Listening	Judgment	Grace
Handwork	Headwork	Analysis	Synthesis
Productivity	Recreation	Specialization	Integration
Intensity	Idleness	Society	Solitude
Serving	Waiting	Laughter	Solemnity
Giving	Receiving	Duty	Freedom
Applying	Learning	Joy	Sorrow
		External life	Internal life[5]

The point of the columns above is that different aspects of life typically have something to balance against. When one side is up, the other is probably down. For example, if you're experiencing a great deal of grief or sorrow in life, you're probably missing out on a measure of joy and happiness. A second example: People may not view someone who exudes a great deal of self-confidence as having an attitude of humility. The trick is to keep some sense of equilibrium between the two sides of the chart.

Balance is seeking that equilibrium in life. It's about finding that sense of stability where the two (or sometimes more) competing tensions find a balancing point.

Perhaps one of the best ways to think about balance is to recall an old-fashioned scale. Maybe you remember using one of these in a math or science class in junior high or high school. Or perhaps you've seen images of the scales of justice. Essentially, this kind of scale features a bar across the top, suspended from or balanced on a single point—a fulcrum. On each end of the bar are platforms to hold the item to be weighed on one side and the countering weights on the other.

To figure out what an item weighs on a scale like this, you set the item on one side of the balance mechanism. Then you place weights on the other side until the scale balances. If you need to know the number of pounds or kilograms or whatever, you simply add up the numbers on the weights themselves.

The scale of justice is often pictured being held by the Lady of Justice. She and her scales symbolize the fair and equal administration of the law, without corruption or favor. Of course, like seeking balance in life, the scales of justice don't always work perfectly! Balance is seeking that equilibrium in life. It's about finding that sense of stability where the two (or sometimes more) competing tensions find a balancing point.

Boil the idea of seeking balance down to its simplest terms. If you sit at a desk and stare at a computer screen all day, you probably shouldn't spend your whole evening at your home computer; for a measure of balance, you might want to do something more physical or active after work. Or, if you have a job or a home life that requires a lot of structure and detail, perhaps your free time needs to be filled with more spontaneous activities. Or, if you have a home business and work alone all day, you need to balance that with some social contacts—even if you just meet a friend for lunch or coffee.

Remember that you can do little things like this to create some sense of balance in your life. But the truth is that you can't truly and completely achieve balance on your own. That can only come from a personal relationship with God through Jesus Christ.

Go back to that picture of the balancing scale. You have to decide where you want to hang your scale. What are your options? Well, you can suspend the fulcrum from the culture around you. But given the culture's ever-shifting nature, that's probably not the most stable place to hang it from. Or you can let someone else hold the scale for you. But do you really want to put your life's balance into some other person's hands? Okay, so maybe it's safest to hold the fulcrum of the scale yourself. But that doesn't sound very easy, does it—both holding the scale and trying to balance everything on it?

You can simply ask God to hold the scale for you.

As a follower of Christ, you have the best solution of all available to you. You can say to God that you know none of the options above will work for very long. You can simply ask God to hold the scale for you. You still have a responsibility— working to balance the weight that lands on one side by trying to balance it with something on the other side.

But with God holding your scale, He can shift the fulcrum of the scale so that balance also comes from Him. Remember moving closer to the center of a teeter-totter as a kid—it took less weight on the opposite end to push you down to the ground, didn't it? God can figuratively apply the laws of physics—or simply defy them if He chooses to—so that you can still feel balance even if you can't muster enough weight to counter the stresses and pressures and weights you're experiencing.

It all happens as you move closer to Him and let Him do the work of keeping your life in balance.

Finding
Balance
in God

A man can no more take in a

supply of grace for the future than he can eat

enough for the next six months. . . . We must draw

on God's boundless store of grace from day to

day.

D. L. Moody

What Does the Bible Say About Balance?

Godliness with contentment is great gain. For we brought nothing into the world, and we can take nothing out of it.

1 Timothy 6:6-7

Okay, are you sick of movie analogies yet? Hopefully not, because you're going to find one at the beginning of each chapter of this book! While movies have been accused of bringing the culture to new lows, sometimes films can provide wonderful contemporary allegories to push your thinking. So allow these movie minutes to jump-start and expand your thinking about balance.

Mr. Holland's Opus follows the teaching career of Glenn Holland, played by Richard Dreyfus, beginning in 1965. Mr. Holland "temporarily" takes a job as a high school instrumental music teacher, planning to earn just enough money to get back on his feet. His real dream is to return to writing his symphony. At first, he hates his teaching job because the students have no interest in music. But as ten, then twenty, then thirty years pass, Mr. Holland is still teaching. When budget cuts end his position and force him to retire, his current and former students perform his symphony—his opus—for the first time. And perhaps for the first time in all those years of teaching, Mr. Holland realizes the influence he's had on hundreds of lives.

At some point in his career, Mr. Holland changes. He stops teaching music in a methodical style and instead tries to instill a love for music in his students. The only way he can do that is through relationships—he begins to care about his students. And without him even knowing it, that's what changes their lives.

Well, the connection between *Mr. Holland's Opus* and this chapter on finding balance in the Bible might seem a bit weak. But it's there. The main point is that God cares for you. He wants to have a relationship with you. And He communicates that through His Word. Beyond that, He wants you to love His Word, not just read it. Through your relationship with God and through your love and study of His Word, you can gain ground in your journey of discovering what a balanced life truly is.

In general, what does the Bible have to say about balanced living?

If you're reading this book from the beginning, you've already read a little bit about how Scripture defines contentment and satisfaction, about how to view the little things in life, and about finding fulfillment. As you continue reading, other sections of the book will continue to look at what the Bible says about different aspects of living a balanced life and how to apply those principles in a practical way.

But specifically, what does Scripture say about balanced living?

> This "economy" of God's seems strange, doesn't it? Yet the same is true for you—your weakness can be a way for God to display His power.

While this passage doesn't use the words "balanced living," the apostle Paul's description of his feelings of joyous contentment in Philippians 4:11-12 certainly sounds like someone who has learned balance in life—even in the face of hardship:

"I have learned to be content whatever the circumstances. I know what it is to be in need, and I know what it is to have plenty. I have learned the secret of being content in any and every situation, whether well fed or hungry, whether living in plenty or in want." Wow! What could this secret possibly be? Paul added verse 13, one that you may have memorized: "I can do everything through him who gives me strength." Or as Eugene Peterson renders this last verse in *The Message:* "I can make it through anything in the One who makes me who I am."

It might help to know a little more about the apostle Paul here. He was writing to the believers in Philippi while under house arrest in Rome. How could he write about being content from whatever meager provisions he had as a prisoner? Of course, Paul hadn't actually been arrested for a true crime; he was only guilty of preaching the gospel message.

But interestingly, instead of stopping or hindering Paul's work, his arrest and detention only furthered the spread of the gospel. In fact, Paul said, "Because of my chains, most of the brothers in the Lord have been encouraged to speak the word of God more courageously and fearlessly" (Philippians 1:14). Imagine how satisfying it must have felt for Paul's mission to be carried on in spite of—in fact, to even benefit from—his imprisonment.

Yet the success of Paul's mission was still not the source of his contentment. Paul was content because of the "secret" he revealed. He explained this secret more fully in another of his letters, one he probably wrote several years earlier to the church in Corinth. In 2 Corinthians 12:9-10 he said, "[The Lord] said to me, 'My grace is sufficient for you, for my power is made perfect in weakness.' Therefore I will boast all the more gladly about my weaknesses, so that Christ's power may rest on me. . . . For when I am weak, then I am strong."

Put even more simply: Paul's human weakness provided the ideal way for God to display His power. This "economy" of God's seems strange, doesn't it? Yet the same is true for you—your weakness can be a way for God to display His power.

He won't just do it; you have to allow Him to. And when you do, that's when you'll sense a supernatural feeling of balance in your life, even when the circumstances around you don't seem very conducive to contentment.

Scripture has many other expressions about what leads to balanced living.

Together, they present another way to think about balancing your life. Psalm 37:4-5 says, "Delight yourself in the LORD and he will give you the desires of your heart. Commit your way to the LORD; trust in him and he will do this." You might be thinking, "Hey, I can be pretty content if God gives me the desires of my heart. Cool!" Before you get too excited, read Philippians 2:13, which answers why God is willing to do this; it's because the desires come from Him: "It is God who works in you to will and to act according to his good purpose." Hebrews 13:20-21 says something similar: "May the God of peace . . . equip you with everything good for doing his will, and may he work in us what is pleasing to him, through Jesus Christ to whom be glory for ever and ever. Amen."

All of these passages seem to indicate that if you seek after God's will, then you'll be in tune with what pleases Him. As you live out His will, He'll give you the things you desire. Those things will be the very things God desires as well. And the result for you is delight and enjoyment of those pleasures, as well as peace, because they come from the God of peace.

To top it off, Ephesians 3:20 says that He "is able to do immeasurably more than all we ask or imagine, according to his power that is at work within us." By seeking and living out God's will, the very desires of your heart will be given to you. And they'll be far more than you can even imagine!

Now that is cool!

According to the Bible, what role does humility — a humble attitude — have in living a balanced life?

One of the best lessons about humility in Scripture comes in the form of a parable that Jesus told: "When someone invites you to a wedding feast, do not take the place of honor, for a person more distinguished than you might have been invited. If so, the host who invited both of you will come and say to you, 'Give this man your seat.' Then, humiliated, you will have to take the least important place. But when you are invited, take the lowest place, so that when your host comes, he will say to you,

'Friend, move up to a better place.' Then you will be honored in the presence of all your fellow guests. For everyone who exalts himself will be humbled, and he who humbles himself will be exalted" (Luke 14:8-11).

Jesus was teaching that if you assert yourself, you'll just defeat yourself. Humility is one of those subjects that doesn't make sense to the world because in many ways, it only works in God's economy.

A Humble Task

I love to accomplish great and noble tasks, but it is my chief duty and joy to accomplish humble tasks as though they were great and noble.

—Helen Keller

If you don't think that statement is true, try explaining these verses to someone who doesn't share your Christian faith:

- Proverbs 22:4: "Humility and fear of the LORD bring wealth and honor and life."
- Matthew 5:5: "Blessed are the meek [humble before God], for they will inherit the earth."
- Matthew 23:12: "Whoever exalts himself will be humbled, and whoever humbles himself will be exalted."
- 1 Peter 5:5-7: "All of you, clothe yourselves with humility toward one another, because, 'God opposes the proud but gives grace to the humble.' Humble yourselves, therefore, under God's mighty hand, that he may lift you up in due time. Cast all your anxiety on him because he cares for you."

While the words humble and humility aren't used in Jeremiah 32:38-41, this brief passage offers a glimpse of what God promises when His children humble themselves. While this prophecy was given to the Israelites, with God promising to return them to their homeland, you can still learn from and claim the spirit of the promise when you humble yourself before God: 'They will be my people, and I will be their God.

Where's Your Nose?

If you walk around with your nose in the air, you're going to end up flat on your face. But if you're content to be simply yourself, you will become more than yourself.

—Luke 14:11, MSG

I will give them singleness of heart and action, so that they will always fear me for their own good and for the good of their children after them. I will make an everlasting covenant with them: I will never stop doing good to them, and I will inspire them to fear me, so that they will never turn away from me. I will rejoice in doing them good."

What does Scripture say about serving God, and how does that relate to balanced living?

The writer of the Old Testament book of Ecclesiastes noted the meaninglessness and folly of work or service that isn't for God. In Ecclesiastes 2:10-11, this teacher spoke of all the pleasures he sought through his work, yet said that none of them brought any real meaning or satisfaction: "I denied myself nothing my eyes desired; I refused my heart no pleasure. My heart took delight in all my work, and this was the reward for all my labor. Yet when I surveyed all that my hands had done and what I had toiled to achieve, everything was meaningless, a chasing after the wind; nothing was gained under the sun."

You might want to argue with this teacher's viewpoint. You might find a lot of satisfaction in your work. You might leave at the end of each day feeling so fulfilled that you can't wait to go back the next day. Look closely at this passage—the teacher said that he also took delight in all his work. But then he said, "yet." It's as if he was suddenly viewing things from a different vantage point. Maybe like Scrooge in the classic story *A Christmas Carol*, the writer of Ecclesiastes saw himself and his hard work from outside himself. And what did he realize? The work he did for himself was meaningless. It meant nothing.

There's probably a reason work is sometimes described as "going back to the grindstone"; perhaps there's some historical explanation for this expression. But think about what a grindstone is—it's a circular chunk of sandstone that revolves on an axle and is used for grinding, shaping, or smoothing. What does that say about the expression "going back to the grindstone"? Could it be that toiling only for yourself is like going around and around and not getting anywhere? Could it be that it's so meaningless that it will grind you down to nothing?

Contrast this word picture with what the apostle Paul said about work in 1 Corinthians 15:58: "Therefore, my dear brothers, stand firm. Let nothing move you. Always give yourselves fully to the work of the Lord, because you know that your labor in the Lord is not in vain."

Paul had just finished describing what a body will look like after being raised from the dead. He

> ### The Power of Serving
>
> It is within my power either to serve God or not to serve him. Serving him, I add to my own good and the good of the whole world. Not serving him, I forfeit my own good and deprive the world of that good, which was in my power to create.
>
> —Leo Tolstoy

was talking about the promise that when those who've committed their lives to Christ die, they'll be raised from the dead and ushered into eternity. And he concluded this thought with the encouragement for Christians to work for the Lord because only work done for God will be meaningful. Laboring for God will mean something—in fact, it will mean everything! It won't feel like a grindstone is wearing you down; instead, you'll know that your effort is a part of God's victory over sin and death.

Your Labor for God

Work for God certainly doesn't mean only full-time ministry of some kind. It means at least two other things:

1. Labor for God includes approaching any job or career with godly principles and Christlike character fully engaged. It means working and conducting business honestly, courageously, lovingly—in other words, applying biblical

principles when it comes to your actions and words, and when your work brings you into contact with other people.

2. Labor for God also includes kingdom work done outside of your job. It means that you bring these same biblical principles to bear as you minister and serve others in the name of Christ.

Does Scripture indicate that serving others has a place in living a balanced life?

Serving others is so interrelated with serving God that it can be difficult to answer this question separately from the previous one. Connected with the idea of working or laboring for or serving God in Scripture is an outward connection with other people. Reread 1 Corinthians 15:58: "Therefore, my dear brothers, stand firm. Let nothing move you. Always give yourselves fully to the work of the Lord, because you know that your labor in the Lord is not in vain." When Paul mentioned "the work of the Lord" in this passage, he was talking about the work and labor of letting others know about His plan to redeem the world.

When you serve God, it means you're involved in telling others of His plan to save mankind from sin and death. When you serve others, it means you're telling them of this redemption plan for mankind. This service to God and others is inseparable.

Ephesians 6:7-8 echoes this intertwining nature of your service: "Serve wholeheartedly, as if you were serving the Lord, not men, because you know that the Lord will reward everyone for whatever good he does."

In another of his New Testament letters, Paul tells of the reward for this service that we do: "May our Lord Jesus Christ himself and God our Father, who loved us and by his grace gave us eternal encouragement and good hope, encourage your hearts and strengthen you in every good deed and word" (2 Thessalonians 2:16-17).

However, like the act of working for God, the deed of serving others will feel empty if you do it for your own gain or reward. Why would you want to do that anyway? Certainly, you can't gain any merit or worthiness with God. It is only when you have the attitude that you're serving God because it's a privilege He's given you—the joy of being a part of furthering His plan for redeeming people—that you receive the reward God promises as a wonderful byproduct.

One Powerful Message

Back in the early 1900s, William Booth, the founder of the Salvation Army, wanted to send a telegraph to the officers of his organization as a Christmas greeting. He wanted to do more than simply greet the officers; he wanted to send a message of Christmas joy as well as encourage them in their humanitarian work and their efforts to spread the gospel message.

When Booth tried to write a message that would be brief enough to be affordable, he struggled with what to say. And as he struggled with what words to use, he also agonized over whether he should even spend the fledgling organization's money to send his message. After much consternation, he finally decided that he would send a one-word message to each of the Salvation Army officers.

That one word? "Others."[1]

One of the key components of finding balance in your service is simply to focus on others rather than yourself.

> **A Fresh Heart**
>
> May Jesus himself and God our Father, who reached out in love and surprised you with gifts of unending help and confidence, put a fresh heart in you, invigorate your work, enliven your speech.
> —2 Thessalonians 2:16-17, MSG

According to Scripture, why do suffering and struggle have to be a part of balancing life? Why do I have to experience pain?

It does seem odd that God allows suffering as part of balancing life. (See also **How does my response to suffering and struggling affect my sense of balance?** on page 86.)

Although you may have read entire books or heard multiple sermons on suffering, maybe no one has ever really answered the questions: "Why do I have to struggle?" and "Why do I have to suffer?"

Why does God allow people to get terminal cancer and die from it? Why does He allow murder to continue? Maybe closer to home, why does He want you to go through financially difficult times? Or why does He allow people into your life who take advantage of you or hurt you emotionally?

Fortunately, Scripture does have a lot to say about this subject. God does have a purpose for allowing you to go through suffering—feelings or effects that range from unpleasantness to discomfort and all the way to grief. Consider what these passages indicate that your suffering produces within you.

Psalm 34:17-18: "The righteous cry out, and the LORD hears them; he delivers them from all their troubles. The LORD is close to the brokenhearted and saves those who are crushed in spirit." God is aware of your suffering and struggles and He understands what you're going through, but you can be assured of one thing if you trust Him completely—*He won't let you go through more than you can handle.*

2 Corinthians 4:7-9: "We have this treasure in jars of clay to show that this all-surpassing power is from God and not from us. We are hard pressed on every side, but not crushed; perplexed, but not in despair; persecuted, but not abandoned; struck down, but not destroyed." In Paul's day, it was customary to hide valuables in clay pots; the idea was that no thief would think to look for treasure in such an ordinary household object. But Paul calls pains and frailties treasures—*because only through your weakness and insufficiency can you experience the strength and sufficiency of God.*

> ### Proved Pure
>
> Pure gold put in the fire comes out of it *proved* pure; genuine faith put through this suffering comes out *proved* genuine. When Jesus wraps this all up, it's your faith, not your gold, that God will have on display as evidence of his victory.
>
> —1 Peter 1:6-7, MSG

Philippians 1:29: "For it has been granted to you on behalf of Christ not only to believe on him, but also to suffer for him." God allows you to suffer because suffering for Him comes with a badge of honor—*to identify you with Christ.*

Philippians 3:10: "I want to know Christ and the power of his resurrection and the fellowship of sharing in his sufferings." The suffering of Christ is something that all Christians can understand and accept, but your own suffering can help you identify and personally experience not only Christ's suffering—*but also the power of resurrection and triumph over death.*

Shaping the Soul

As for the battle that ends tonight, I do believe as my father once said, that no matter how hard the loss, defeat might serve as well as victory to shape the soul and let the glory out.

—Al Gore, in his concession speech in the 2000 presidential election[2]

Hebrews 12:7: "Endure hardship as discipline; God is treating you as sons. For what son is not disciplined by his father?" God isn't a mean or domineering Father. He's a loving Daddy. And your "discipline" is proof of something wonderful—*that God loves you as His very own child.*

Hebrews 12:10: "God disciplines us for our good, that we may share in his holiness." Your hardships occur to make you holy—*refined from the impurities of sin.*

Hebrews 12:11: "No discipline seems pleasant at the time, but painful. Later on, however, it produces a harvest of righteousness and peace for those who have been trained by it." What you learn from your painful experiences can provide great benefits—*an upright and peaceful life of balance.*

Strength

What doesn't kill me makes me stronger.

—Albert Camus

James 1:2-3: "Consider it pure joy, my brothers, whenever you face trials of many kinds, because you know that the testing of your faith develops perseverance." You can easily fill in the blank for this purpose that you might have to suffer or struggle—*to develop perseverance.*

1 Peter 2:23: "When they hurled their insults at him, he did not retaliate; when he suffered, he made no threats. Instead, he entrusted himself to [God] who judges justly." When we suffer for the sake of Christ, we learn to respond to pain as Christ did—*without seeking revenge or retaliating.*

The Last Word

Keep a firm grip on the faith. The suffering won't last forever. It won't be long before this generous God who has great plans for us in Christ—eternal and glorious plans they are!—will have you put together and on your feet for good. He gets the last word; yes, he does.

— 1 Peter 5:9-11, MSG

Revelation 21:3-4: "Now the dwelling of God is with men, and he will live with them. They will be his people, and God himself will be with them and be their God. He will wipe every tear from their eyes. There will be no more death or mourning or crying or pain." While struggles may go on during your whole life, and you'll suffer the pain and reap the benefits of becoming more like Christ—*in the end, ultimate victory over sin and death belongs to Christ, and God Himself will wipe away the tears from your eyes!*

What does Scripture say about finding comfort when life seems out of balance?

The Bible is amazing. In it, God communicates directly with us through the written word. Jesus communicated the same message in the flesh during His earthly life. The Holy Spirit lives within each believer to instill that message in us. And then there's

God's Word—direct communication from God that you can study and apply in your daily walk with Him.

And like many other circumstances you face in life, God isn't silent about His willingness to comfort you during the trying times of life. Look at these passages and rest in the comfort that only God can provide.

Deuteronomy 4:29-31: "If from there you seek the LORD your God, you will find him if you look for him with all your heart and with all your soul. When you are in distress and all these things have happened to you, then in later days you will return to the LORD your God and obey him. For the LORD your God is a merciful God; he will not abandon or destroy you." When you seek God with all of your being in the good times, you'll know exactly where to find Him when you need His comfort. And you have His promise that in His mercy, He'll provide you with the comfort you need.

Zephaniah 3:17: "The LORD your God is with you, he is mighty to save. He will take great delight in you, he will quiet you with his love, he will rejoice over you with singing." God is like a loving, patient, and proud parent. When you become His child, He shows you off with great delight, He comforts you with His love when you need it, and He shows joy in you to the extent that He can't contain Himself and even bursts forth in song!

2 Corinthians 1:3-4: "Praise be to the God and Father of our Lord Jesus Christ, the Father of compassion and the God of all comfort, who comforts us in all our troubles, so that we can comfort those in any trouble with the comfort we ourselves have received from God. For just as the sufferings of Christ flow over into our lives, so also through Christ our comfort overflows." The comfort you receive from God is so amazing that it allows you to offer comfort to others. God will give so much comfort that it will spill out of you and into the lives of people around you who need comforting.

2 Corinthians 5:18-21: "All this is from God, who reconciled us to himself through Christ and gave us the ministry of reconciliation: that God was reconciling the world to himself in Christ, not counting men's sins against them. And he has committed to us the message of reconciliation. We are therefore Christ's ambassadors, as though God were making his appeal through us. We implore you on Christ's behalf: Be reconciled to God. God made him who had no sin to be sin for us, so that in him we might become the righteousness of God." As God's ambassador, you can offer His reconciliation, restoration, and fulfillment to those around you who need it.

Inherently Worthful

Every individual is inherently worthful to the Father—every child everywhere, of every race, of every condition. Love requires response, and parenthood craves companionship and cooperation. Therefore every human being on this globe is indispensable to God, indispensable in the sense that God can never be fully Himself without loving comradeship, and He can never complete His work without faithful cooperation from every individual everywhere. . . .

Jesus knew men to be frail, sinful, easily corrupted, sometimes monstrously depraved, capable of cruel and atrocious behavior—but always, always, always a child of God, and, even when a prodigal, indispensable to the lonely and yearning heart of the Father.[3]

What specifically does Christ say about living a balanced life?

Jesus understood the idea of discontentment. Not that He gave in to the temptation to try to fill up His life with external things. But as a man, He would have been tempted to try to find balance on His own, apart from His relationship with His Father. Hebrews 4:14-15 says, "Therefore, since we have a great high priest who has gone through the heavens, Jesus the Son of God, let us hold firmly to the faith we profess. For we do not have a high priest who is unable to sympathize with our weaknesses, but we have one who has been tempted in every way, just as we are—yet was without sin."

Aside from the Bible telling us that He experienced every kind of temptation, you can be certain Jesus knew what it felt like to be out of balance, to feel empty. Otherwise, He wouldn't have offered people a way to fill up their lives. "Because he himself suffered when he was tempted, he is able to help those who are being tempted" (Hebrews 2:18).

What Jesus suggested about balance and fulfillment probably sounded just as strange to those who listened to Him in person as they might sound today. He didn't suggest plans, programs, conferences, retreats, or even a book for those looking for balance. Instead, here's what He said in John 6:35: "I am the bread of life. He who comes to me will never go hungry, and he who believes in me will never be thirsty." Jesus wasn't talking about food and water here. He was addressing the sense of imbalance and discontentment that people have in their hearts. Jesus knew that God designed human beings to be satisfied when they have a personal relationship with Him. He sent Jesus to earth to die and be raised from the dead as part of His plan so that anyone who wants to can have a relationship with Him. Without this personal relationship with God through Jesus Christ, you can't ever truly feel in balance, you can't truly know what contentment feels like, and you can't truly have that emptiness in your heart go away. Sure, you can do things to feel okay for a while (those conferences, plans, programs, and so on.). These external forces might help you feel happy for a time. You could certainly gain a sense of satisfaction for a brief period. But without a personal relationship with God, those good feelings go away and you have to chase them down again.

Jesus also said, "As the Father has loved me, so have I loved you. Now remain in my love. If you obey my commands, you will remain in my love, just as I have obeyed my Father's commands and remain in his love. I have told you this so that my joy may be in you and that your joy may be complete. My command is this:

Make Yourself at Home

"I've loved you the way my Father has loved me. Make yourselves at home in my love. If you keep my commands, you'll remain intimately at home in my love."

—John 15:9-10, MSG

Love each other as I have loved you. Greater love has no one than this, that he lay down his life for his friends. You are my friends if you do what I command. . . . I have called you friends, for everything I learned from my Father I have made known to you" (John 15:9-15).

Though we don't always think of these verses in this way, Jesus was talking about balance here, too. Maybe it's a bigger picture than finding balance day to day. But true balance in daily life flows from feeling a sense of fullness and balance in your overall life.

It's interesting that Jesus said "remain in my love." What did He mean by that? Picture a plant on a shelf in your house. If a leaf falls off or you pluck it off, what happens to the plant? It most likely goes right on living. But what happens to the leaf? Apart from the plant, it dies. If you remain in Jesus' love—through a personal relationship with Him—you'll have a sense of purpose and fulfillment in life. Life won't be perfect. But feeling useful and having a sense of purpose will help carry you through the tougher times as you desire to see both what God is teaching you and what awaits you after the tough times.

Even during difficult times, Jesus offers a sense of peace that also leads to a feeling of balance in life. In John 16:33 He said, "I have told you these things, so that in me you may have peace. In this world you will have trouble. But take heart! I have overcome the world."

Only Jesus can offer true peace, a true sense of balance. Anything the world offers will be a poor imitation. There's no example that describes the difference between the quality of peace Jesus offers and the knock-off version the world offers. In a small way, maybe it's like the difference between handmade leather shoes that are made precisely to fit your feet versus those off-the-shelf shoes made of manmade vinyl that your parents bought you as a kid. Those cheap shoes caused blisters because they were mass-produced and they just weren't made to fit you properly. When it was cold outside, the vinyl got stiff and your feet got cold and grew even more uncomfortable.

But the wonderful hand-sewn leather shoes—they conform to every contour of your foot and almost become an extension of your own skin.

You can probably see where this analogy is going. The peace the world offers is easy. It's mass-produced. But in essence, you get what you pay for. The peace Jesus offers is unaffordable. You can't pay any price on your own to have it. But amazingly, God gives it to you. Jesus Himself bought it for you. You just have to accept the gift.

How does my relationship with God play into feeling balanced in life?

Your relationship with God is an awesome thing, isn't it? It's complete. Unlike human relationships, which can only offer one or two facets that you need, God offers you everything: He's a loving parent and you're His child. He's a loving master and you're His servant. He's a tender shepherd and you're one of His flock. He's a righteous judge and you're the receiver of His mercy. He's the attractive bridegroom and you're part of the church, His bride.

God is all these things and so much more than our human words can describe or our human minds can understand. He is complete, and He offers all that He is to you in His relationship with you.

What's funny is that if you sometimes make choices that don't honor your relationship with God, you're certainly not alone. Scripture itself is filled with real-life stories of people who knew God, yet often chose to head a direction opposite of the way He was pointing them. And the fabric of the history of the church is also woven with stories of people who went their own way for a time rather than God's way.

When it comes to finding balance, you're probably no different than the heroes of the

> **Not in Your Wildest Dreams!**
>
> God can do anything, you know—far more than you could ever imagine or guess or request in your wildest dreams! He does it not by pushing us around but by working within us, his Spirit deeply and gently within us.
> —Ephesians 3:20, MSG

Accomplishment

I myself do nothing.
The Holy Spirit
accomplishes all through
me.

— William Blake

---

faith in Scripture or the saints who make up the history of the church. But the best part of your relationship with God is that He knows you want to veer off course. Imagine Him asking you directly, "What is that one thing that you think will make you happy in life? Name it—money, fame, stature, pleasure." Now imagine the conversation with God continuing when He asks, "Is that really better than what I have to offer you?"

In His relationship with you, God offers you so much more than you can ever dream of for yourself. Isaiah 40:10-11 says, "See, the Sovereign LORD comes with power, and his arm rules for him. . . . He tends his flock like a shepherd: He gathers the lambs in his arms and carries them close to his heart." Wow! What a wonderful illustration of who God is! All at once, He's sovereign, strong, gentle, and loving. How could we ask for more than that in our relationship with Him?

Yet He offers even more! Ephesians 3:16-19 says, "I pray that out of his glorious riches he may strengthen you with power through his Spirit in your inner being, so that Christ may dwell in your hearts through faith. And I pray that you, being rooted and established in love, may have power, together with all the saints, to grasp how wide and long and high and deep is the love of Christ, and to know this love that surpasses knowledge—that you may be filled to the measure of all the fullness of God." Amazingly, He is more than you can imagine, *and* He will give you more than you can even think to ask for.

Don't settle for second best. When God asks, "What is that one thing that you think will make you happy in life? Name it—money, fame, stature, pleasure," answer, "I know that only You will make me happy God, because You'll provide more than I can ever imagine."

Does prayer play a role in feeling balanced?

Your prayers are simply your direct conversation with God. You can talk to Him any time. The apostle Paul wrote, "Pray in the Spirit on all occasions with all kinds of prayers and requests" (Ephesians 6:18).

Even when you don't know what to pray, the Holy Spirit steps in to make sure that God hears your prayers. Romans 8:26-28 says, "In the same way, the Spirit helps us in our weakness. We do not know what we ought to pray for, but the Spirit himself intercedes for us with groans that words cannot express. And he who searches our hearts knows the mind of the Spirit, because the Spirit intercedes for the saints in accordance with God's will. And we know that in all things God works for the good of those who love him, who have been called according to his purpose." The Spirit not only steps in when you can't find the right words to express yourself, He also ensures that you're praying for God's will!

> **Mingling Tears**
>
> Prayer is the way to both the heart of God and the heart of the world—precisely because they have been joined through the suffering of Jesus Christ. . . . Praying is letting one's own heart become the place where the tears of God and tears of God's children can merge and become tears of hope.
>
> —Henri Nouwen[5]

Whole books have explored the intricacies of prayer. Yet the basic concept of prayer remains simple: "In everything, by prayer and petition, with thanksgiving, present your requests to God" (Philippians 4:6).

Why pray? "To pray is to change," wrote Richard Foster. "If we are unwilling to change, we will abandon prayer as a noticeable characteristic of our lives. The closer we come to the heartbeat of God, the more we see our need and the more we desire to be conformed to Christ."[4]

With that goal of being conformed to Christ in mind, here are some simple ways you can focus on prayer:

Using your daily planner or calendar. Keep a list of prayer requests and answers and move those pages ahead from day to day or week to week. Or divide your list into different topics on different days. For example, Mondays pray for family members, Tuesdays for friends, Wednesdays for people who are ill, Thursdays for your own personal needs, Fridays for community and government leaders, and so on.

Walking through your neighborhood or workplace. As you go past neighbors' houses or coworkers' desks, silently pray for these people's needs.

While exercising. This could be a great time to pray for your own health, and to ask God to heal people you know who are sick or injured.

As your kids leave for school each day. Pray for the safety and God's protection of your own children and their classmates, for them to honor God in their studies and schoolwork, as well as for teachers and school administrators.

While gardening, mowing, raking, shoveling snow. Not everyone loves these tasks, but you can improve your attitude by thanking God for how He sustains you.

During household chores. You'll certainly feel more content as you spend time thanking God for a comfortable place to live; and a spouse, family, and good friends you can build relationships with.

When the phone rings. Say a quick prayer as you run to answer the phone (or doorbell). Use a device like this to remind you throughout the day of a request you want to repeatedly bring before God.

As you get ready for the day. As you shower, towel off, and get dressed, ask God to bless you and your time as you serve Him and others in the day that lies ahead.

What Do You Pray For?

Nine out of ten adults say they pray. What do they pray for the most?

98 percent—their own families

81 percent—the world's children

77 percent—world peace (apparently, those bumper stickers are working!)

69 percent—coworkers

61 percent—their enemies

48 percent—the U.S. president[6]

Balance

from

Believing

The greatest battle of our

spiritual lives is not "Will you try harder?" or

"Can you make yourself worthy?" It is "Will you

believe?"

Jim Cymbala

Why Do Things Seem Out of Balance?

*Outwardly we are
wasting away,
yet inwardly we are
being renewed
day by day.*

2 Corinthians 4:16

In the special-effects-filled movie *The Matrix*, Keanu Reeves plays Thomas Anderson—an ordinary guy in an ordinary life in what he thinks is the year 1999. At night, Anderson is a computer hacker who goes by the name of Neo.

A man named Morpheus shows up and explains to Neo that his late-twentieth-century world is a kind of virtual reality. The true reality is actually 200 years later, after the world has been destroyed and taken over by advanced artificial intelligence. The twentieth century's virtual reality is called "the matrix," and it exists just to keep human slaves deceived and satisfied about their meager existence. Morpheus explains the matrix to Neo: "You feel it when you go to work, or go to church, or pay your taxes. It is the world that has been pulled over your eyes to blind you from the truth."

Not that long ago, you might have thought the idea of a story like the one told in *The Matrix* was such a farfetched tale that you'd have found it hilariously ridiculous. But maybe now you're not so sure—because in today's world, sometimes it's tough to tell what's real and what isn't.

Seeking balance in life can feel nearly as elusive as reality. In fact, balance may seem even more enigmatic because balance and contentment are something you want every day—"when you go to work, or go to church, or pay your taxes." Yet balance so easily escapes us. Just when you think you've got your arms around what balance is, life throws another curveball at you and once again, you're "off balance."

This chapter explores some of the reasons that life can so easily seem out of balance. While the answers sometimes offer brief ideas, exercises, and advice about how you can start to regain some balance in your life, you'll find much more of that practical help later on pages 129-172.

Why is it so easy to feel discontent?

It's pretty difficult to continuously and simultaneously manage all the demands of life—both internal and external—to keep life in balance. When you think you should be able to keep the plates spinning or keep a few more balls in the air as you juggle your responsibilities and commitments, think of Joseph Odhiambo, who holds the world record for dribbling the most basketballs simultaneously. Even he can only dribble five basketballs at one time.[1]

Our capacity to effectively manage multiple events and aspects of life is more limited than we like to think. It might help to remember that even the most experienced psychologists and counselors, the most educated pastors and philosophers, and the most vaunted and valued leaders of the business world all struggle with feelings of discontentment just like you do. It's not something to be alarmed about; in fact, it's part of how God created us.

Think of a time when you were sick—maybe with just a cold. You could eat, but with your head all stuffed up and your throat rough and raw, the foods just didn't taste very good. Then, a few days later, when you were feeling much better—maybe as you were enjoying one of your very favorite foods—you suddenly realized just how wonderful food tastes again. Wow! It's as if every taste bud in your mouth is now working overtime, making up for time missed when you were sick. At first, this rediscovered sense of taste is so wonderful that you shovel your food in as fast as you can. Then you realize that you're not tasting every bite, so you slow down, savoring each food's taste and texture—even aroma. As you put a bite into your mouth, you pause for a minute with the food under your nostrils, letting the wonderful smell waft up for just a fleeting second. Then you put the food in, allowing each and every bite to roll over your tongue so that you don't miss a single bit of flavor.

> The old saying that "the grass is always greener" is something that everyone feels at one time or another.

Discontentment in life is a lot like your cold. The positive side is that when you get beyond it, the feelings of contentment taste a lot better because you suddenly recall how bland everything was when you felt so discontented. Every part of you revels in the early tastes of contentment.

Of course, your human nature will eventually pull on you, seeking ways for you to feel discontent again. This is much like how your earthly body again becomes susceptible to new viruses and bacteria that give you new bouts of illnesses which take away that wonderful taste and make you miserable otherwise.

That's a fairly long analogy for what boils down to a simple truth: Everyone feels discontent at some point. The old saying that "the grass is always greener" is something that everyone feels at one time or another: "If only I had more money, then I could get out of debt and be happy." "If only my children/spouse/employees/coworkers would give me more respect." "If only I had a bigger house." "If only I could get a new car/couch/computer/cell phone/you name it!"

You've probably fallen prey to the "if only" game. It's easy to play when you're not content with life. Remember that true contentment can only come from a fulfilling personal relationship with God through Jesus Christ. Remember how the apostle Paul described this: "I have learned to be content whatever the circumstances. I know what it is to be in need, and I know what it is to have plenty. I have

The Recipe for Happiness

I've found the recipe for being happy whether full or hungry, hands full or hands empty. Whatever I have, wherever I am, I can make it through the One who makes me who I am.
—Philippians 4:12-13, MSG

learned the secret of being content in any and every situation, whether well fed or hungry, whether living in plenty or in want. I can do everything through him who gives me strength" (Philippians 4:11-13).

Before these verses in his letter to the Philippian Christians, Paul talked about all the blessings of his life—qualities that are available to all believers—that allowed him to feel content. After these verses, Paul expressed his appreciation for the Christians in Philippi, and for their concern for him. You might even say that rather than focusing on what he didn't have, writing from his house arrest in Rome, he focused on all that he did have—both because of his vertical relationship with God, and his peer or horizontal relationships with fellow believers.

That's something you can do just as easily. You can follow the advice of that old hymn, "Count your blessings, name them one by one." You can make a mental list if you'd like, but you might feel even better emotionally—and move toward that savory time of feeling content—if you actually take a pen and paper and write down the positive aspects of your life.

Here are some positive big-picture blessings for you to focus on:

- When was the last time you thanked God for putting you where you are— with your family, your work, your areas of ministry? List as many connections in your life that you can think of, including family relationships, work, and so on. Write down a promise or a vow that you'll pray for effectiveness—asking God to show you precisely how He wants you to be effective in each area— each day for the next two weeks. You can certainly continue to pray for the same thing well beyond the first two weeks, but commit to praying *every day* for two weeks as an exercise to decrease your feelings of discontentment.

- Make a list of your strengths. Rather than thinking about tasks you're good at, think about what qualities and skills you have that transcend the different hats you wear at home, work, church, and in other involvements. For example, if you're a good listener no matter where you are, write that down. If you're adept at arbitrating and peacemaking, list that. Beside each quality, include examples of how you've been able to demonstrate each one. Then ask God to give you additional opportunities—in all areas of your life—to use your strengths. One month later, return to your list and make notes about how God has used the positive qualities and strengths you've listed.

- Make another list of significant ways you've influenced other people's lives in the past year. The list might include quantities ("The small group I lead at church added three new couples last year and is ready to birth a daughter group") or qualities ("My spouse and I have grown closer because we started praying together on March 1 of last year"). Now, list new areas where you'd like to have an impact on people's lives.

- Spend time praying, thanking God for the opportunities you hadn't recognized until now, and asking Him to provide new opportunities for you to serve Him and feel fulfilled.

- Honestly evaluate if you give credit where it's due. For the next two months, commit to thanking and affirming—using specific words and descriptions—at least three people a week for ways you see them serving others. This is especially important in areas that intersect your life or where someone might think you've been the servant. Affirming them specifically means that you might say to a co-worker, "I really appreciate how you helped Sandi catch up with her reports when she returned from maternity leave" rather than just a curt "thank you." As part of this exercise, thank God at least three times a week for giving you the blessing of touching other people's lives.

> **Other Voices**
>
> Discontentment comes in my life when I fail to trust that God is always doing the right thing at the right time. When things happen that I have no control over, I have to learn that God is still in control. Without that perspective, feeling discontent is inevitable.
>
> —Steve

At the end of each of these exercises—two weeks, one month, and two months—evaluate how you're feeling about yourself. Do you feel more content, more fulfilled? Where is this feeling coming from? If you can honestly answer that God is helping you feel this way, be sure to give Him thanks for that as well.

Note how most of these have to do with you, but also with serving others. Often, you'll feel discontent when you focus inwardly on yourself. By focusing on others and how you can serve them, you'll oddly feel more content with your own life—not by realizing how bad others have it in life, but by recognizing and acknowledging how good you have it in life.

How does a sinful nature—a fallen world—prevent me from having a sense of balance in my life?

By its simplest definition, the term "sinful nature" means missing the mark—the ideal that God set for humans when He created us. It's like an inherent material defect in a part of your new car—the defect is just there when the car rolls off the factory assembly line and still there when you drive it off the showroom floor. You didn't cause the defect; it came with the car.

The sinful nature in you is the same way. And just like when you receive a recall notice to go have the defective part replaced on your new car, God asks you if you want a new nature to replace your earthly and sinful nature. If you don't heed the recall on your new car, and you decide to keep driving with a defective part in your engine, you might do huge damage, which then you are responsible for. In the same way, if you don't replace the sinful nature within you, it will eventually control you. Your sinful nature is what keeps you from not being able to resist sin on your own.

Even the great apostle Paul struggled with possessing an inherent human nature that was the root of his sin. He commiserated in Romans 7:14-15, "We know that the law is spiritual; but I am unspiritual, sold as a slave to sin. I do not understand what I do. For what I want to do I do not do, but what I hate I do."

Paul was saying that your sinful nature and your weak flesh can never measure up to God's standards on your own. Your own strength will always fail you, and like Paul, you'll exclaim, "I don't understand what I do," even when you really want to do the right thing. This nature within you creates internal anxiety, indifference, and chaos.

(By the way, biblical scholars disagree if Paul is speaking here of sin before he became a follower of Christ, or if he is still struggling with his fallen and sinful nature after he became a Christian. In some ways, it doesn't matter, because the point of Paul's teaching here is that no one has to choose to live under the oppression of a sinful nature.)

Fortunately, Paul went on in Romans 8 with a big old "therefore" to describe the solution or antidote to this sinful nature. Rather than battling it and trying to overcome it yourself, you have to accept what God did for you when Christ died on the cross: "Therefore, there is now no condemnation for those who are in Christ Jesus, because through Christ Jesus the law of the Spirit of life set me free from the law of sin and death" (Romans 8:1-2).

The Law in the Old Testament meant condemnation for those who didn't live up to it. Like laws of our day, violation of the laws brought a consequence or sentence. The violation of God's law meant death. But in the New Testament—the New Covenant or contract with God—those who are in Christ are set free from the law of sin and death: "You have not come to a mountain that can be touched and that is burning with fire; to darkness, gloom and storm. . . . You have come to God, the judge of all men . . . to Jesus the mediator of a new covenant" (Hebrews 12:18,23-24). You come before God, who because He embodies justice, demands a penalty. But He also provides the payment of the penalty through His mercy—the New Covenant provided through Jesus' shed blood on the cross. It's like receiving a pardon from a death sentence you've been given. Or you might think of it more like a prisoner exchange, because Jesus paid the death penalty that God required, and in return, you are set free from the law and its death penalty.

How does all this relate to balance? In its most simple terms, the struggle within you that sin creates feels anything but balanced—it might feel stressful, confusing, or you might not even care how it makes you feel. But when you ask God to replace those feelings with His Spirit, instead you can experience a general sense of peace and freedom.

This peace and assurance come from knowing that, for Christians, God sees your penalty or fine for breaking His law as already paid in full. Certainly, it still grieves Him when you fall prey to your sinful nature. To understand that a little better, you might think of what it would feel like if you gave an extremely rare and precious gift to someone, and as soon as you handed him the beautifully wrapped package, instead of saying thanks, he spit in your hand. Oh, sure, he gladly took the gift. But his words and actions indicated that he didn't appreciate the gift.

God might feel that way if you go on sinning after you've received the gift of Jesus Christ. That's where those uneasy, stressful, and unbalanced feelings come from—knowing that your sin will make you feel more distant from God. But it isn't God putting the distance between Himself and you. You've put that distance there.

The good news is that you have what Scripture often calls "a hope." You might use the word promise instead. Others may call it assurance. Whatever you call it, it's God clearly assuring you that He is the way He is and He tells you exactly how He will deal with you. God is like a loving parent, always waiting with open arms for you to move closer, to move back into His presence, back into His open and waiting arms. Romans 5:1-2 lists some of the ways we have assurance from God: "Since we have been justified through faith, we have peace with God through our Lord Jesus Christ, through whom we have gained access by faith into this grace in which we now stand. And we rejoice in the hope of the glory of God."

Peace with God—You've become His child, He's your loving Father, and you no longer need to feel separated from Him.

Access to God's presence—Your relationship through Jesus Christ allows you to communicate directly with God.

Grace—You receive God's favor and love, even though on your own you don't deserve it at all.

Glory of God—This phrase is often used to mean roughly, "what God intended you to be, and is now creating or restoring in you."

How do my own sins hinder me from finding balance in life?

Because you enter this world with a sinful nature (see the previous question), you can try all you want to do the right thing, but you'll still end up committing sin. That's why it's called a "nature." It's like the "nature" that parents have to protect their children. An even better example is that it's so inherent in you that it's like eating or breathing—sin is something you might even do without thinking because it's so basic to who you are as a human being. One of the most memorized and most quoted verses in the Bible is Romans 3:23: "For all have sinned and fall short of the glory of God."

Maybe you can't fathom this and are thinking to yourself, *It's not fair that I can't help it if I sin or not; I didn't ask to be born with this horrible defect—a sinful nature.* Then these words might be more convincing: "If we claim to be without sin, we deceive ourselves and the truth is not in us. . . . If we claim we have not sinned, we make [God] out to be a liar and his word has no place in our lives" (1 John 1:8,10).

At its very root, sin is something that keeps you separated from God. Whether that separation occurs because of an inherently sinful nature or because you choose to commit specific sins doesn't really matter. What does matter is that you can't have a relationship with God with sin in your life. But it's the sin in your life that keeps you from having a relationship with God. What a dilemma. And of course, without a relationship with God, you won't have true balance in life either.

Well, the positive in all of this discussion about sin is that God can provide the strength you need to stop sinning. Oh, you'll still sin, maybe even every day. But God will both make you aware of your sin and help you work on getting that sin out of your life.

What are some ways God can help you stop sinning? Take a look at a few Scripture passages that might help you understand.

Psalm 66:18: "If I had cherished sin in my heart, the Lord would not have listened." Cherish means to love and adore something. One way to stop sinning is to work on loving God more than you love whatever sin it is you're committing. This might seem to be true just for the everyday sins that you repeat, such as lying, gossiping, or saying hurtful things. But it will work just as well for any sin that tends to dominate and make you feel separate from God—if you really determine to love God more than the sin.

Psalm 119:9: "How can a young man keep his way pure? By living according to your word. I seek you with all my heart; do not let me stray from your commands. I have hidden your word in my heart that I might not sin against you." This verse is often quoted as a reason to memorize Scripture. And there's nothing wrong with that at all. But simply memorizing Bible verses doesn't do any good. Remember that God's Word is one source of clear and direct communication from God. And as you learn and apply His Word, you can stay pure—free from moral and ethical wrongdoing.

Other Voices

My human nature wants to satisfy its own desires at any cost. It constantly demands more. Sin prevents anything good in my life. Satan doesn't want me to try to find my balance in God. He wants me to search for it among the lies that he feeds me. Only when God has control of my life do I find contentment. He loves me more than anyone—even myself—and He only wants the best for me.

—Robert

1 Corinthians 10:13: "No temptation has seized you except what is common to man. And God is faithful; he will not let you be tempted beyond what you can bear. But when you are tempted, he will also provide a way out so that you can stand up under it." Being tempted isn't the same as sinning. Even Jesus was tempted by Satan, yet Jesus didn't sin. It's when you give in to temptation that you sin. However, God doesn't let you face more temptation than you can handle. And He'll provide a way for you to resist the temptation so that it won't turn into sin.

Hebrews 12:1: "Therefore, since we are surrounded by such a great cloud of witnesses, let us throw off everything that hinders and the sin that so easily entangles, and let us run with perseverance the race marked out for us." The "therefore" that begins this verse refers to the previous chapter of Hebrews, where the writer told of great heroes of the faith. They were examples both of what it means to live in faith and to trust God who is always faithful. These heroes are meant to inspire you to overcome your sin with God's help.

Victory Over Sin

Romans 6:11-13 provides three steps to help followers of Christ achieve victory over sin:

1. "Count yourselves dead to sin" (verse 11). Accept that you are dead to sin and alive to God, and in faith, you live in light of this truth.
2. "Do not let sin reign in your mortal body" (verse 12). Refuse to let sin be in control of your life.
3. "Offer yourself to God" (verse 13). When tempted to offer your body to sin, instead put yourself in service to God.[2]

Seven Losses When You Sin

1. The loss of light—1 John 1:6
2. The loss of joy— Psalm 51:12; John 15:11; Galatians 5:22; 1 John 1:4
3. The loss of righteousness—1 John 3:4-10
4. The loss of love—1 John 2:5,15-17; 4:12
5. The loss of fellowship—1 John 1:3,6-7
6. The loss of confidence—1 John 3:19-22
7. The possible loss of health and even physical life—1 Corinthians 11:30[3]

How does my response to suffering and struggling affect my sense of balance?

On pages 61-63, we looked at why suffering, struggle, and pain are a part of balancing life according to Scripture. But maybe you're still confused about exactly how you're supposed to respond to suffering. How can something that seems to make you weaker—at least while you're going through it—actually give you a sense of strength and balance?

Before you can seek balance through the hard times of life, you have to understand that you have a choice about what will result from the struggles you face. Once you grasp that, and make the choice that you want to allow your suffering to make you a more godly, Christlike person, then you can look for how balance comes through trials and hardships. Again, Scripture offers some amazing insights into how your suffering and trials shape you.

Jeremiah 29:11: "'I know the plans I have for you,' declares the LORD,' plans to prosper you and not to harm you, plans to give you hope and a future.'" You might not always understand the specific trial you're going through or why you're going through it, but peace and balance come from trusting God's overall plan for you and your life. *His plans and purposes for you and for His kingdom are worked out in intricate detail, including through suffering.*

2 Timothy 2:20: "In a large house there are articles not only of gold and silver, but also of wood and clay; some are for noble purposes and some for ignoble. If a man cleanses himself from the latter, he will be an instrument for noble purposes, made

---

Constant Risk

What they did to Jesus, they do to us—trial and torture, mockery and murder; what Jesus did among them, he does in us—he lives! Our lives are at constant risk for Jesus' sake, which makes Jesus' life all the more evident in us.

—2 Corinthians 4:10-11,
MSG

holy, useful to the Master and prepared to do any good work." Because it is a refining act (cleansing), your suffering sets you apart (makes you holy). *This process makes your service to God useful for carrying out His work.*

2 Corinthians 4:16-17: "Therefore, we do not lose heart. Though outwardly we are wasting away, yet inwardly we are being renewed day by day. For our light and momentary troubles are achieving for us an eternal glory that far outweighs them all." No matter how difficult life and its struggles may be, when you look at your suffering in the perspective of all eternity, the weight of your struggles can also be put into perspective. *Still to come is a life beyond what you can imagine, and you'll receive blessings that never end.*

Worthy of Love?

The great temptation is to use our many obvious failures and disappointments in our lives to convince ourselves that we are really not worth being loved. . . . But for a person of faith the opposite is true. The many failures may open that place in us where we have nothing to brag about but everything to be loved for. It is becoming a child again, a child who is loved simply for being, simply for smiling, simply for reaching out.

—Henri Nouwen

These words in 2 Corinthians provide another important thing to keep in mind. As followers of Christ, you have received and will receive many gifts from God. To begin with, the joy and privilege of having a relationship with Him is a gift from Him. As you know, a gift is something that the giver gives freely, without any strings attached. But like all relationships, your relationship with God goes beyond that initial gift. As it deepens, one of His desires for you is that you develop Christ-like character. While a gift is immediately yours as soon as you accept it, character is developed over time, with repeated and deepening experiences that infuse that character into who you are. When that godly character saturates your very being and then radiates from you, then you have grasped what it means to have balance

in your life. Then, no matter what life throws at you, you react with godly character. It comes out of you because it's been refined in you. You prove it by the way
you respond.

Ephesians 4:14-15 provides another word picture of what happens in this
process of increasing in character: "Then we will no longer be infants, tossed back
and forth by the waves, and blown here and there by every wind of teaching and by
the cunning and craftiness of men in their deceitful scheming. Instead, speaking the
truth in love, we will in all things *grow up* into him who is the Head, that is, Christ."

Balance means examining what kind of ship you are. Are you tossed back and
forth by the waves of suffering and pain? Or does your refined godly character
allow you to sail across the water whether the sea is calm or rough?

The Father of Reconciliation

Maybe you not only feel pain from trials and suffering that you've faced, but you
specifically feel hurt by the church or by an individual who claims to be a Christian.
Of course, your hurt is real. But 2 Corinthians offers hope for finding healing and
fellowship in God's family once again.

- God—through the power of the gospel—can transform your life, no
  matter what your hurts are: "You yourselves are our letter, written on our
  hearts, known and read by everybody. You show that you are a letter from
  Christ, the result of our ministry, written not with ink but with the Spirit
  of the living God, not on tablets of stone but on tablets of human hearts"
  (2 Corinthians 3:2-3). God is inviting you to let Him heal you, transform
  you, and live through you.
- No matter how much you hurt, God doesn't want you to give up:
  "Therefore, we do not lose heart. Though outwardly we are wasting away,
  yet inwardly we are being renewed day by day" (2 Corinthians 4:16).
  However you hurt because of what someone said or did to you, God can

amazingly use that very hurt to renew you! In spite of whatever guilt or unworthiness you feel, you can be a new creation. "If anyone is in Christ, he is a new creation" (2 Corinthians 5:17). The pain and suffering that lie in the past are hurts that Christ can help you understand, deal with, forgive, and leave in the past.

- You may feel hurt by God because someone connected with God has hurt you. But God is in fact the inventor of restoration and reconciliation: "God was reconciling the world to himself in Christ" (2 Corinthians 5:19). God isn't an abusive parent; rather, He loves you so much that He sacrificed Christ to repair and restore the relationship He wants to have with you. You have to make the choice to accept His gift to you.

- Why wallow in your hurt even another minute? "'In the time of my favor I heard you, and in the day of salvation I helped you.' I tell you, now is the time of God's favor, now is the day of salvation" (2 Corinthians 6:2). God is a loving and patient parent, and you can reestablish your relationship with Him at any time. But why waste even one more day feeling the way you do? Accept His gift now.

Do bad habits, addictions, and other negative behaviors affect how balanced my life feels?

This is a big question. Whole books have been written about overcoming addictions. There's a whole area of ministry and counseling called the Recovery Movement that deals with breaking bad habits, overcoming addictions, and changing negative behaviors. So what you read in these few paragraphs may not be enough to help you with even the most minor of these problems, let alone the more serious ones.

The biggest problem with negative behaviors and addictions is that they keep you from balance by hindering your relationship with God. The behavior or addiction simply comes between you and God. God is there, patiently waiting, knowing that He's already offered you His forgiveness and a relationship with Him if you'll simply accept it. But guilt, pleasure, pride, feelings of unworthiness, or whatever may be stopping you from saying, "I'm sorry, God, please forgive me. I want to be close to You as You've promised so that I can live for You."

Beyond that, in spite of any gratification these actions might bring—highs from illegal drug abuse, relief from life's pressures from alcohol overuse, and physical pleasures from sexual addictions—choosing these behaviors is really like settling for second best or less. You do them because they probably bring some pleasure. Or at the very least, they provide an escape from troubles or hardships or suffering. But Jesus said, "No one can serve two masters. Either he will hate the one and love the other, or he will be devoted to the one and despise the other" (Matthew 6:24). The apostle Paul echoed this thought in his letter to the believers in the Roman church: "Don't you know that when you offer yourselves to someone to obey him as slaves, you are slaves to the one whom you obey—whether you are slaves to sin, which leads to death, or to obedience, which leads to righteousness" (Romans 6:16).

In other words, anything you choose before God—including addictions and negative habits and behaviors—is what you become a slave to. You may have heard an alcoholic describe his addiction as totally controlling him. Drug addicts will use all their savings, sell their possessions, and alienate themselves from their families just to get another fix. That's the worst kind of bondage!

Paul went on with the good news about overcoming this slavery to addictions or bad habits: "Thanks be to God that, though you used to be slaves to sin, you wholeheartedly obeyed the form of teaching to which you were entrusted. You have been set free from sin and have become

The Reward of Loyalty

Anyone who meets a testing challenge head-on and manages to stick it out is mighty fortunate. For such persons loyally in love with God, the reward is life and more life.

—James 1:12, MSG

slaves to righteousness" (Romans 6:17-18). By choosing to follow Christ, obeying Him, and relying on His strength, you can be set free from negative behaviors. To believe differently, you're denying that Christ has the power to change you through His love and grace. Your other "master"—the addiction or behavior you're involved in—will lie to you, telling you that Christ doesn't have that kind of power and authority.

But as Paul assured followers of Christ in the Galatian church, "It is for freedom that Christ has set us free. Stand firm, then, and do not let yourselves be burdened again by a yoke of slavery" (Galatians 5:1).

If you're still reading, it's possible that you

> ## A God-Fashioned Life
>
> That old way of life has to go. It's rotten through and through. Get rid of it! And then take on an entirely new way of life—a God-fashioned life, a life renewed from the inside and working itself into your conduct as God accurately reproduces his character in you.
>
> —Ephesians 4:23-24, MSG

might have a serious problem with an addiction. You're searching for *the* answer. *Christ* is *the* answer, but you might need more help to grasp how He can help you. Don't be too proud or ashamed to talk to a pastor or a Christian counselor in your cry for help.

But it's also possible that you're simply nodding your head, agreeing with everything here, but thinking that you don't really have a problem with any kind of addiction, negative behavior, or bad habit. "I don't use drugs." "I don't have multiple sexual partners outside my marriage." "I don't drink excessively." Fill in the blank with whatever you've been thinking as you've read these words. Then ask yourself, "But is there anything I do to keep myself from experiencing emotions I don't want to deal with?" "Is there something that I'm trying to escape from?" "Is there something I turn to again and again because it makes me feel good?"

Before you answer, think about what those things might look like. Do you shop beyond your means because it's a way to anesthetize yourself to how you really feel? Do you work long hours to avoid investing in your relationship with your spouse or children? Do you watch excessive amounts of television and movies to escape your own reality of life?

These might not seem like addictions or negative behaviors in the traditional sense. But what these have in common with more immediately harmful behaviors is that you probably choose them because they keep you from feeling bad—either about yourself or the circumstances you're in. The difference is that these less extreme behaviors seem neutral. You can reason them away: "What's wrong with getting away from it all sometimes? Is there really any harm in escaping from life occasionally?"

> God doesn't want you to choose bad. And He doesn't want you to choose "just okay." He wants you to experience the best life possible.

Here's another way to think about it: Choosing the severe behaviors is like choosing between good and bad. That very distinction between good and bad might make it easier for you to not cross the line because the boundary itself is so much bigger and bolder and clearer. But deciding to cross the line to these everyday escapes isn't such a clear choice. The boundary is often much fuzzier and grayer. Instead of choosing between good and bad, you're making the choice to have something that is second best rather than choosing the best. Again, the apostle Paul put words around this thought when he wrote, "This is my prayer: that your love may abound more and more in knowledge and depth of insight, so that you may be able to discern what is best and may be pure and blameless until the day of Christ, filled with the fruit of righteousness that comes through Jesus Christ" (Philippians 1:9-11). God doesn't want you to choose bad. And He doesn't want you to choose "just okay." He wants you to experience the best life possible.

Of course, that will bring balance to your life, because you're making the choice for God's best for you. This isn't easy. It's not a "magic wand" event. It's a process, an ongoing choice that leads to God's best as you grow closer to Him in relationship and more like Him in character. Paul describes this process in Romans 12:1-2: "Therefore, I urge you, brothers, in view of God's mercy, to offer your bodies as living sacrifices, holy and pleasing to God—this is your spiritual act of worship. Do not conform any longer to the pattern of this world, but be transformed by the renewing of your mind. Then you will be able to test and approve what God's will is—his good, pleasing and perfect will."

Every time I think about better times in my life, I realize how out of balance life seems right now. How can I deal with those memories of "the good old days"?

It's kind of funny to think about the old days as good. While not all the news of the past has been bad, it's much easier to romanticize the good old days and not remember the negative events that impact history just as much as the positive events and advances.

Every decade in the past century has had its set of big problems, and probably decades before that did as well. Look at this list, and maybe think about when you were growing up. Ask yourself if the good old days were really that good, or were they just old?

1910s—World War I began, communist reign began in Russia, Prohibition began.

1920s—Mussolini, Hitler, and Stalin began rising to power, the Stock Market crashed, Saint Valentine's massacre occurred in Chicago.

1930s — The Great Depression was triggered by the 1929 Stock Market crash, Nazis gained power in Germany, Hitler acquired dictatorial powers, Prohibition repealed, Amelia Earhart disappeared.

1940s — The Holocaust, Pearl Harbor attack pulled U.S. into World War II, U.S. dropped atomic bombs on two Japanese cities, People's Republic of China (Communist China) and German Democratic Republic (East Germany) established.

1950s — Cold War era began, five U.S. congressmen shot in House of Representatives, Castro seized control of Cuba.

1960s — Cuban missile crisis, U.S. pulled into Vietnam conflict, JFK assassination, Watts riots, racial and civil rights violence, Martin Luther King Jr. assassination, Robert F. Kennedy assassination, Woodstock music festival held.

1970s — Kent State shootings, mandated school busing, Watergate scandal, Arab terrorists killed eleven Israeli athletes at Olympics, mass cult suicide in Guyana, oil shortages, Iran hostage crisis, Three-Mile Island nuclear power plant accident.

1980s — Air controller strike, space shuttle Challenger explosion, Chernobyl nuclear power plant accident, Iran-Contra affair, Pan-Am 747 explosion caused by terrorist bomb killed 270 people.

1990s — Persian Gulf War, rise of AIDS, O. J. Simpson trials, Branch Davidians and Waco, presidential sex scandal and impeachment hearings, school shootings.[4]

This list might make you wonder what wonderful times the twenty-first century will bring!

Because the good old days aren't really as good as you might remember, it's no wonder that the wise writer of Ecclesiastes advised, "Do not say, 'Why were the old days better than these?' For it is not wise to ask such questions" (Ecclesiastes 7:10). Isn't it great that hundreds of years before Christ was born, the writer of Ecclesiastes was advising God's followers not to ask the same question we're still asking? Who says Scripture—including the Old Testament—isn't relevant today?

Well, wishing for a return of the good old days might be something you desire on a more personal level. Maybe you remember something wonderful about when you were growing up. Maybe it was a childhood event. Some people romanticize about high school so much that they never really leave it, wearing their letter jackets and leaving their hair cut the same way for years! But chances are—if you really think about those days that you remember so fondly—you also went through some terrible times as well.

> ### Unshakable, Assured
>
> "I've told you all this so that trusting me, you will be unshakable and assured, deeply at peace. In this godless world you will continue to experience difficulties. But take heart! I've conquered the world."
>
> —John 16:33, MSG

One reason people are so fond of the past is that it's a known factor. What the future holds is unknown. If you're anxious about the future, you're certainly not going to have a sense of balance in your life. Remember the words in Matthew 6:27: "Who of you by worrying can add a single hour to his life?" Later in that same chapter is verse 34: "Do not worry about tomorrow, for tomorrow will worry about itself. Each day has enough trouble of its own."

Giving up the good old days and having a sense of balance and security about the future comes from trusting in God for His plan both for you personally and for His "big picture" plan for eternity. Here's what Jesus said about the future: "I have told you these things, so that in me you may have peace. In this world you will have trouble. But take heart! I have overcome the world" (John 16:33). Jesus announced this to His disciples right before His crucifixion. What an awesome moment for Him to make His rightful claim of victory! He was saying that it doesn't matter what happens in the events of life. What matters instead is that the final chapter of God's story is already written, and God is completely victorious over Satan at the end.

Jesus also said, "Peace I leave with you; my peace I give you. I do not give to you as the world gives. Do not let your hearts be troubled and do not be afraid" (John 14:27). This passage is becoming very familiar to you by now. But it's repeated here because it indicates that you have a choice—the fear and trouble that the world gives when the future is unknown, or trusting in Christ and experiencing His peace.

Balance comes from loving God, demonstrating your love by obeying what He's asked and commanded you to do, and trusting Him for your future (actually, even trusting Him and relying on Him are part of His command). First John 5:3 affirms this: "This is love for God: to obey his commands. And his commands are not burdensome, for everyone born of God overcomes the world. This is the victory that has overcome the world, even our faith. Who is it that overcomes the world? Only he who believes that Jesus is the Son of God." By trusting God, you can have balance in your life both day to day and in the perspective of eternity.

The Practice of Balance

What would a violin solo sound like if the strings on the musician's instrument were all hanging loose, not stretched tight, not disciplined?

A. W. Tozer

Going After Balance

*I urge you . . . to offer your
bodies as living sacrifices
holy and pleasing to
God — this is your
spiritual act of worship.*

Romans 12:1

In the movie *Parenthood*, Steve Martin plays Gil Buckman, a modern-day man who badly wants to maintain a successful career while also struggling — nearly to the point of exhaustion — with wanting to be a better dad than his own father was. All around Gil are his immediate and extended family, and the movie poignantly and humorously tells the story of their relationships, their ups and downs, and their battles to find happiness in life and in parenthood.

Near the end of the movie, Gil's grandma remembers her younger years and makes a pithy observation about life. She recalls going to an amusement park when she was nineteen. "Grandpa took me on a roller coaster," she recalls. "Up, down. Up, down — oh, what a ride. You know, it was interesting to me that a ride could make me feel so frightened, so scared, so sick, so excited, and so thrilled all together." She remembers that some people went on the merry-go-round instead, but she wonders aloud, "What fun would that be? It just goes around. I like the roller coaster — you get more out of it."

In one of the movie's final scenes, as Gil frets over yet another thing that he can't control as a dad, the floor under his feet begins to undulate like a roller coaster. At first, Gil looks almost sick — he certainly isn't enjoying the ride at all. Then he looks at his wife, who's always had a way of just enjoying what life brings, and she's laughing and loving the ride. Gil finally relaxes and enjoys the ride, laughing with the people around him, and loving whatever life brings.

Finding balance in life is like that in many ways—you can worry about everything and resist all the circumstances life throws at you. Or you can surrender those things to God and allow Him to put balance in your relationship with Him, with your family, with coworkers, with people in your community of faith, and so on.

The purpose of this section is to look at various places in people's lives in which they search for balance, and to try to determine whether seeking balance in those areas is the best way to discover true balance. You may bump into some of these same topics later in **Seeking Balance in Your Own Life,** (starting on page 127), but the emphasis will be less on if it's *possible* to find balance in these areas, and more on *how to apply* the concept of balance to these.

In the meantime, enjoy the roller coaster ride! You'll get more out of it.

Can I achieve balance in my relationships? Can other people help me find balance in life?

Of course, having other people involved in your life can certainly help you find a sense of balance. Getting outside of yourself is nearly always a good idea. Healthy relationships with friends, coworkers, spouses, and family members can all lend a sense of balance to your life.

However, if you go looking for balance in your relationships in a selfish way— looking to take but not give—you're likely to do serious damage to your relationships. If you abuse the relationships too much, you're probably going to lose them altogether. Except for the most committed family members, most people aren't going to be involved in too many relationships that aren't somewhat equal. That doesn't mean you can't ever rely on someone more than they rely on you for a time. But over the course of the relationship, you're probably going to have to let the scale tip back the other way for a while. Not that friends and family members should keep score, but you may need to let others lean on you a little more heavily sometimes when you've leaned on them for a while.

Our culture doesn't necessarily have the same view of relationships that Christians do. If you ever watch daytime television talk shows, you know that the relationships depicted are typically not equal. Perhaps those relationships aren't the best examples of what goes on in most relationships—let's hope not. But, unfortunately, these shows and what they depict do represent at least some segment of society. These relationships seem to be based on what one person can get out of his or her friends or even family members. You might even hear something like, "Why should I waste my time on someone who won't do anything for me when I'm entitled to so much more than that?" These people seem to have the attitude that there's always someone else to take advantage of.

The Bible has a lot to say about how Christians should conduct themselves in relationships. Entire books have been written—and because it's so important, many more will be written—on friendships, workplace relationships, family relationships, marriage, and parenting. If you've been involved in churches for very long, you've probably heard a lot of preaching and teaching about all of these relationships as well.

But here's a Top Ten list of some general principles you can use to guide your relationships, based on what are sometimes called the "one anothers" of the New Testament. Live this way in your relationships and you're likely to sense a lot of balance in your life when it comes to the people you touch and who touch you on a regular basis.

1. "Love one another." This is first because it's the basis for all the others, and it's the most often mentioned "one another" in the New Testament. Jesus uttered these words to His disciples just shortly before His crucifixion, saying, "A new command I give you: Love one another. As I have loved you, so you must love one another" (John 13:34). Imagine what your own relationships would look like if you loved the people around you in the unselfish and sacrificial way that Jesus demonstrated love during His earthly life and ministry. Imagine what churches would look like if the people in them loved one another this way. Imagine the kind of influence Christians would have on our culture if the world saw them loving one another like this. You can read a lot more about loving one another by following Christ's example and because of His love for you in 1 John 3 and 4.

2. "Honor one another above yourselves" (Romans 12:10); "in humility consider others better than yourselves" (Philippians 2:3). This theme is another concept that Christ exemplified. He honored others—even common sinners, the most hated government officials, and the outcasts of His day. And it was the ultimate humility for the Son of God to die on the cross even though He was totally blameless and free from sin. The thought here for you is to treat the people you have a relationship with as Christ would treat them.

Even if you're the most introverted, quiet person ever, having authentic and peaceful relationships will attract people to you.

3. "Be at peace with each other" (Mark 9:50). Again, these words were spoken by Jesus Himself. Sometimes it's easy to get so wrapped up in the stories about Jesus and the teaching He did in parable form that you can forget to listen to specific instructions He gave to His disciples that in turn are given to you in Scripture. If you have peaceful relationships as a follower of Christ, you'll have an extremely strong witness to the world. Even if you're the most introverted, quiet person ever, having authentic and peaceful relationships will attract people to you because they'll see that you're a good friend.

4. "Accept one another." Romans 15:7 tells why: "Accept one another, then, just as Christ accepted you, in order to bring praise to God." Again, Christ is mentioned as the example for the boundaries of what you should accept. During His earthly life, Jesus associated with some pretty worldly people. He didn't condone their lifestyles (in fact, He often pointed out what was wrong with their actions), but He nevertheless loved them. In fact, think about who you were before you became a

Christian—were you living a lifestyle worthy of Christ's love? Of course not. The old saying that you should "hate the sin but love the sinner" is probably a pretty good guideline here. Accept the people you have relationships with as they are. Don't try to change them. Transforming them is God's job, not yours (Romans 12:2).

5. "Instruct one another" (Romans 15:14); "admonish one another." Colossians 3:16 says, "Let the word of Christ dwell in you richly as you teach and admonish one another with all wisdom." If your life is filled with the world's ideas about what relationships are supposed to be like, that's what's going to come out of you. If your life is filled with what God's Word says, that's going to drive your relationships. Scripture is calling you to the latter—taking in God's Word to the extent that you can approach your relationships wisely.

6. "Serve one another" (Galatians 5:13). First Peter 4:10 says, "Each one should use whatever gift he has received to serve others, faithfully administering God's grace in its various forms." God doesn't give you spiritual gifts to be used selfishly. He expects you to use your gift or gifts to minister to others.

Spiritual Gifts

- Prophecy—proclaiming God's principles to edify others
- Serving/Ministry/Helps—doing for others and meeting needs
- Teaching—understanding difficult matters and making instruction understood
- Exhortation—persuading, encouraging, inspiring
- Giving—undergirding and supporting
- Leading/Administration—organizing and inspiring cooperation and teamwork
- Mercy—showing concern and caring for those who are hurting
- Wisdom—applying truth and understanding to life situations
- Knowledge—understanding facts and situations
- Faith—inspiring others to have confidence in the Lord

- Discernment—making judgments about good or evil and seeing beyond the surface of a situation
- Evangelism—witnessing in any situation and talking easily about Christ
- Hospitality—desiring to unselfishly meet the needs of others
- Speaking—showing interest in others, talking easily with them, and inspiring them
- Celibacy—remaining single to devote even more time to God's work[1]

7. "Carry each other's burdens" (Galatians 6:2). The idea here is that if you're a follower of Christ, you'll care so much for the people you touch that you'll willingly and humbly walk alongside them when they're struggling. Further, you'll do this without any sort of superior attitude, realizing that at any time you might be facing a trial, dealing with a hardship, suffering from grief, or reeling from giving into a temptation. You act as Christ's hands and feet, carrying another person's burden—all with the attitude of that old saying, "There but for the grace of God go I."

8. "Be patient . . . with one another." This instruction for relationships comes from Ephesians 4:2: "Be completely humble and gentle; be patient, bearing with one another in love." Humility and a soft touch, as well as patience, should mark your relationships. Patience means not giving up on your friends and family. It might even

> ## Marks of a Friend
>
> Agree with each other, love each other, be deep-spirited friends. Don't push your way to the front; don't sweet-talk your way to the top. Put yourself aside, and help others get ahead. Don't be obsessed with getting your own advantage. Forget yourselves long enough to lend a helping hand.
>
> —Philippians 2:2-4, MSG

include practicing unconditional love when someone wrongs you.

9. "Be kind and compassionate to one another, forgiving each other" (Ephesians 4:32); "forgive whatever grievances you may have against one another" (Colossians 3:13); "stop passing judgment on one another" (Romans 14:13); "don't grumble against each other" (James 5:9); "don't lie to each other" (Colossians 3:9). Obviously, this list is more than a single "one another." But it includes a number of mostly negative behaviors that you can watch out for in your relationships. If you're not forgiving your family members, if you're passing judgment on your friends, or if you're grumbling about a coworker behind her back—these and other behaviors are signs that your relationship is unhealthy in some way. Correct the behaviors to make the relationship healthy and balanced. This might not be easy, but you're directly disobeying God if you don't discipline yourself to correct the problem.

> ### Desire for Friendship
>
> Oh how important is discipline, community, prayer, silence, caring presence, simple listening, adoration, and deep, lasting faithful friendship. We all want it so much, and still the powers suggesting that all of that is fantasy are enormous. But we have to replace the battle for power with the battle to create space for the spirit.
>
> —Henri Nouwen

10. "Encourage one another and build each other up" (1 Thessalonians 5:11). God puts us in relationships with other people for this very reason. You can encourage and build up others by reminding your friends and family how much they mean to you (and God), how much you care for them (as does God), and how you appreciate having a relationship with them (God wanted this relationship with His children so much that He sacrificed His Son). Tell others specifically what you appreciate about them. Tell them ways you've seen them serve others and God, and affirm them for giving their time or talent to further God's kingdom.

What about finding balance in what I do — my actions, my work, and so on?

Often, what you do for a living or choose for a career contributes to your self-esteem. Your work says a lot about your interests, your talents, and your personality. Considering how much the Bible has to say about work, God certainly ordained it.

Here are some facts about work based on Scripture:

God works. "Indeed, he who watches over Israel will neither slumber nor sleep" (Psalm 121:4); "Jesus said to them, 'My Father is always at his work to this very day, and I, too, am working.'" (John 5:17)

Work allows you to give to the needy. "He who has been stealing must steal no longer, but must work, doing something useful with his own hands, that he may have something to share with those in need." (Ephesians 4:28)

Your work is for God. "Serve wholeheartedly, as if you were serving the Lord, not men, because you know that the Lord will reward everyone for whatever good he does." (Ephesians 6:7)

Work is a place where you can live out and speak of your faith. "Be wise in the way you act toward outsiders; make the most of every opportunity. Let your conversation be always full of grace, seasoned with salt, so that you may know how to answer everyone." (Colossians 4:5-6)

Work provides for your own needs. "For even when we were with you, we gave you this rule: 'If a man will not work, he shall not eat.' We hear that some among you are idle. They are not busy; they are busybodies. Such people we command and urge in the Lord Jesus Christ to settle down and earn the bread they eat." (2 Thessalonians 3:10-12)

Work provides for your family. "If anyone does not provide for his relative, and especially for his immediate family, he has denied the faith and is worse than an unbeliever." (1 Timothy 5:8)

This overview of how God sees work demonstrates in a general way that, like in other areas of life, you can certainly seek balance in your work. (For some hands-on, practical, day-to-day ways to find balance as you do your work, see **How can I find balance in my work?** on page 135.)

A brief word of caution about work, especially if you have the type of personality that drives you toward workaholism: Be sure to balance work—or any overly dominant area of life—with other spheres of life. Check yourself if you begin to sacrifice family, church, leisure, or any other aspect of life for working.

How do the media and the culture affect how I view balance?

Unless you live in a cave or hut without electricity on the world's most remote deserted island, the media and culture probably influence you to some degree. And even if you have completely withdrawn from society and are living the life of a recluse, you've now been exposed to some tastes of the culture in this book. Sorry! The point here is that as you observe success, happiness, and prosperity—as well as how people handle failures, depression, and poverty—in television shows, movies, books, and even news stories, it's pretty likely that your view of balance in life will be affected.

Of course, not all of these influences are negative. If you want to deny that any positive things are going on in the world, then you're essentially saying that the church and Christians have no influence at all on society. Of course, that isn't true, because even our society's laws and basic moral standards are based on Scripture. And Christians continue to have a voice in shaping what our culture looks like.

However, many things that go on in our culture *are* negative. So the key is to learn the art of discernment—figuring out what's good, what's bad, and what's neutral. And then you can move beyond discerning to apply the good to your own life, to shun or try to change the bad, and to positively influence the neutral.

So what is discernment and how do you get it?

One way to think about discernment is to remember two other words that begin with *d*: *discover* and *determine*. To discern whether any person, place, or thing is good, bad, or indifferent, you first need to *discover* all that you can about it. The idea is to investigate, explore, and expose any relevant facts. Once you've done that, you can then *determine* its influence on you. This means applying your values and standards— which as a Christian should be increasingly godly standards and characteristics— to check whether it's a good influence, a bad influence, or simply not a factor.

As you observe success, happiness, and prosperity—as well as how people handle failures, depression, and poverty—in television shows, movies, books, and even news stories, it's pretty likely that your view of balance in life will be affected.

The culture can also affect your sense of balance if you let it dominate in another way. If you are so concerned about the culture that you shun it completely, you run the risk of losing important relationships and your witness to those around you.

How could that happen? Well, maybe you grew up being taught that it was a sin to go to a movie theater, dance, or play pool. You may still feel uncomfortable doing any of those things, and that's fine. But your choice not to participate in these activities doesn't have anything to do with sinning or your salvation. And it certainly doesn't have to do with anyone else's sin or salvation—at least that's not up to you to decide. You have to separate what's essential to the Christian faith from the things that arise out of your own personal background or tradition.

Think about the apostle Paul. When he traveled to different cities in the Roman Empire in the first century, he spoke to the citizens of each region with an understanding of their cultures. In Athens, for example, while it distressed him to see that the city was full of idols, he walked around and looked at their objects of worship and found an altar to "an unknown god." Rather than demand that the Athenian citizens destroy all of their idols, he used the unknown god as a point of contact, explaining that he knew this god. While some of them sneered and jeered Paul, others invited him back to speak again (see Acts 17).

Of course, in today's culture you'll first want to use your discernment about whether you should be in a certain situation. And you'll want

> ## Discernment
>
> *Discover* all you can about the possible situation you're facing. Investigate, explore, and expose any relevant facts.
>
> Then *determine* its influence on you applying your godly values and standards to decide whether it's a good or bad influence, or simply not a factor.

to ask God to help you make good decisions that reflect Him and His character. But at the same time, if you remove yourself from the culture to the degree that you become unaware of what's going on in the world, you won't have much of a contact point with the people you know. It's important to remember that God loves even the most sinful and vile people, and He wants them to enter into a personal saving relationship with Him.

Of course, there is a line you probably don't want to cross. But that line may be pretty gray—especially in terms of whether other Christians should cross the line you draw for yourself. You may not want to listen to rock music, but be thankful and pray for Christians involved in that industry who can have a godly influence on people you might see as evil. You may not want to see motion pictures, but thank God for Christian movie makers, producers, lighting experts, makeup artists, and the like who demonstrate God's love to people in that business. You may think the news media is too liberal for your tastes, but be grateful for journalists, news producers, camera operators, and others who have a daily influence on the people who make up that industry.

What's the role of community and church in helping me find balance?

If you go to your local Christian bookstore, you're likely to find a good number of books that have been written about small groups, care groups, and cell groups. Your pastor probably has a lot of these titles on his or her shelf, and has probably attended a conference or workshop about starting or strengthening a small group ministry. And small groups *are* great. Many do help group members recognize the elements that Scripture points to for living a balanced life. As author Kevin Graham Ford writes, "Human beings . . . crave connectedness and meaning, we seek lasting and deep relationships, we grow by sharing and not keeping secrets, and we need to trust and be trusted in order to feel safe." When small groups accomplish these things, they're wonderful.[2]

But what if you've sincerely made an attempt to be involved in a small group, yet for some reason, the concept or the structure or the particular groups you've tried haven't worked for you? Where can you turn if this intimate form of community hasn't worked?

Two answers: (1) Try again, and (2) look for the same kind of support in unconventional places. There's no right way to do small groups. They don't have to be based on some cookie-cutter approach. In fact, the best groups are ones that seem to arise somewhat organically, rather than being programmed.

If you feel burned out for the time being with church groups, at the very least use and increase your involvement in support networks you might already have in place. These could include extended family, Christian friends from work, close friends who might still be close even though you're separated geographically, neighbors you're close to, or a service or volunteer group. The key—at least in terms of seeking balance in your life—is to connect beyond a superficial level with a group of people who can support you when you're down, and whom you can support when they're down. Balance in a group typically comes from this kind of give and take.

If you don't have access to any of these kinds of groups (or even if you do), you should also keep trying with church small groups. When they work, church small groups are great places to connect with people who share your faith, beliefs, and values. They're places where you can talk about what's weighing you down without the other group members rejecting you because you lack faith. These groups are places where you can be yourself and where you allow others to be themselves. If your congregation doesn't have this kind of ministry or it doesn't seem very successful, talk to your pastor about how to get something going or how to improve on what's there. If that isn't possible, don't be afraid to find a church that emphasizes the importance of care groups in some way.

I've heard a lot about accountability. Do I need a friend or group to help me seek balance?

Accountability is all about integrity. In Matthew 12:33-37, Jesus said, "Make a tree good and its fruit will be good, or make a tree bad and its fruit will be bad, for a tree is recognized by its fruit. You brood of vipers, how can you who are evil say anything good? For out of the overflow of the heart the mouth speaks. The good man brings good things out of the good stored up in him, and the evil man brings evil things out of the evil stored up in him."

Accountability is evidenced by your integrity. Your integrity is demonstrated by the way you act or speak. This means that what you do and say reveals what's in your heart. While you might be able to "fake it" for a while, eventually what's in your heart will be seen in your words and actions. Accountability is the idea of no longer trying to fake it, but to have another person or a group of people get to know you well enough to check what's in your heart, and to help you change it if necessary. And balance in your life will come from that—you won't be wasting precious time and energy trying to be on the outside what you think people around you want you to be, when on the inside you're really nothing like that at all.

Of course, the transformation of your heart is impossible without a relationship with Christ. Remember the process described in Romans 12:2? "Do not conform any longer to the pattern of this world, but be transformed by the renewing of your mind." Only Christ can truly carry out the process of transforming you and your heart. He will likely use the people around you as His arms and hands and legs and feet. The first step is found in Romans 12:1: "I urge you, brothers, in view of God's mercy, to offer your bodies as living sacrifices, holy and pleasing to God." You need to surrender your heart wholly to God so that the transformation can begin. Then you need to allow Him to change you.

Holding Yourself Accountable!

Sometimes whether you're "doing the right thing" ends up being between you and the One you can't hide anything from—God. The acronym for *accountable* provides a way to think about holding yourself accountable to God in your life, your relationships, and your areas of service.

A—Accept that your life isn't your own. If you have to be in control of every little thing in your life, is it possible that you're not trusting God? Pray for God's will to be done in your life and for Him to make you content by working in and through you.

C—Choose a friend. Or choose several people that can hold you accountable. The act of looking someone in the eye who will confront you honestly and firmly (yet lovingly) will keep your actions and words honest and honorable.

C—Consequences. Like children (which we are of God) we tend to learn best when we face consequences for the wrong actions we take. If you do fail to hold yourself accountable, force yourself to pay some kind of penalty. Don't let yourself get away with wrestling control back from God. Ask the friends you chose in the C above to help you enforce your discipline.

O—Others first. This is a simple way to begin being accountable: Treat people with the respect you want to be treated with. You'll be amazed how much more patience you'll have when you put the opinions of others—your coworkers, family, those you're involved with at church—before your own.

U—Unity. The apostle Paul said that Christ's followers will possess "compassion, kindness, humility, gentleness and patience. . . . And over all these virtues put on love, which binds them all together in perfect unity" (Colossians 3:12,14). Nothing creates a sense of balance more than feeling like you're part of a team accomplishing meaningful purposes.

N — Nobility. The idea here isn't kingly at all; in fact it's far closer to humility and humbleness. Scripture calls us to fill our minds and meditate "on things true, noble, reputable, authentic, compelling, gracious — the best, not the worst; the beautiful, not the ugly; things to praise, not things to curse" (Philippians 4:8, MSG). The result of this kind of thinking is revealed in verse 9: God's peace.

T — Teamwork. In spite of seminar leaders in the eighties getting rich leading workshops on this topic, it's really nothing new. In fact, God invented this concept. Moses needed his big brother Aaron to be an effective leader. The apostle Paul needed people around him like Barnabas, Silas, and Timothy. Be a part of a team that shares God's vision — whether it's your coworkers, your family, or a committee at church.

A — Affirm. Part of holding yourself accountable to God includes not tearing down those around you. Even if you disagree with what someone says, affirm the person who says it.

B — Be bold. This may sound counter to being humble, but this has to do with those times in your life when you're extremely clear — no doubts at all — about something God wants for you, your work, your family, or your church. If you're positive that your motives are pure, go for it! Boldly move to the next step. This is also a part of holding yourself accountable to God and His leading.

L — Love unconditionally. You'll feel out of balance if you hold grudges against what someone says or does. God loves you unconditionally and holds you account-able to do the same if you expect to sense His peace and contentment.

E — Enjoy life. Use this litmus test: Whatever situation you're in, stop and think about how important your decisions and relationships will be five or ten years from now. Some things are worth fighting for, but you'll be much more content in life if you don't make every little skirmish into a major world war.

Like the small group movement, whole movements within Christianity have grown out of the idea of accountability partners and groups. And again, some very positive things have come out of those organizations and ministries: parents become better parents, spouses become better husbands and wives, followers of Christ become more like Him.

But again, not every Christian fits the mold that the accountability movement has created. If you do fit, and an accountability partner or group helps you find balance, that's great. But if you're the type who doesn't fit into molds very well, then maybe your spouse, a long lost friend from the past, or a parent might work better for you. Just remember that whether a traditional accountability relationship fits you or you need to find some alternative, you're looking for relationships with people who God will use to help your heart and life to be transformed.

What about celebration? Doesn't celebrating life's little victories bring balance?

The quick answer to this question is "yes." Celebrating after the "wins" of life and even appropriately commemorating the "losses" of life can help you bring balance. Marking occasions in a special way tends to help the lessons you've learned and the circumstances you've experienced sink in. Do you remember every mundane detail of every mundane day? Or do you tend to remember the big events? Celebrating and commemorating some of the little events has a way of turning them into more memorable occasions.

As a Christian, you do this regularly with God (or at least you're probably trying to). Worshiping God is a way of celebrating who He is and what He does for you. This kind of celebration is a way of regularly demonstrating that you know God has done and is doing important things for you, recognizing that He loves and cares for you, and acknowledging that above all, He deserves your worship and praise. You may do this alone, quietly, on a daily basis, but when you

> **Worship**
>
> Celebrate God all day, every day. I mean, *revel* in him!
> —Philippians 4:4, MSG

go to a corporate church service, you also are celebrating in a bigger way so that you don't take your relationship with Him for granted. Corporate worship is one of those "make it memorable" ways of celebrating.

At first, it might seem a little awkward to focus on celebrating the little victories—and even the defeats—of your life. But once you get the hang of making these events more memorable, you'll find that you feel a lot more content about life. This is similar to being grateful for everything God provides, but it's taking that concept to the next level and saying, "I'm so grateful for this that I'm going to celebrate it and remember it."

> ### Your Well-Being
>
> Always leave enough time in your life to do something that makes you happy, satisfied, even joyous. That has more of an effect on well-being than any other single factor.
>
> —Paul Hawken

What are some things you can celebrate? This list is just for starters: birthdays, anniversaries, job promotions, your children's good grades, a new house, a new baby, graduations, starting a new job. Celebrate by: going out to dinner, having a spontaneous get-together with cake and ice cream, planning a surprise party, going to the beach or mountains or lake.

You might also celebrate some of the smaller things: getting the whole house cleaned, painting a room, your child finishing his homework. These call for smaller celebrations, but still mark the occasion by: having a fudge bar around the family dinner table, going out for a latte or cappuccino, fixing a favorite meal.

You can also celebrate—or at least commemorate in some way—the less enjoyable times of your life that you suspect may have something to teach you. Again, this is simply to help you better remember the events when God reveals to you what the struggle was all about. For example, when someone dies, a funeral is a way for friends and loved ones to honor that person's life and to pay respects. Funerals are also a time to process what has happened. A funeral may be a time when you realize what someone's friendship meant to you personally. Or when you at least mentally list qualities or characteristics of the person who died and what those things meant to you, your family, your church, your place of employment, or your community.

Preciousness of Life

Celebration is possible only through the deep realization that life and death are never found completely separate. Celebration can really come about only where fear and love, joy and sorrow, tears and smiles can exist together.
Celebration is acceptance of life in a constantly increasing awareness of its preciousness. And life is precious not only because it can be seen, touched, and tasted, but also because it will be gone one day.

—Henri Nouwen

You can certainly observe difficult times in your life that may be slightly less significant than someone's death. These times might include losing a job, a divorce, a child going off to college (this could be a positive experience for the child, but it might be the start of a depressing time for you), a foreclosure of property or a bankruptcy, a change in living conditions, a change in work hours or conditions. Because these aren't really celebrations in the way you usually think of that word, you need alternative ways to observe them. So instead of a party, you might mark the occasion differently by: writing a psalm that describes how you feel about an event; videotaping yourself talking about the circumstances of the event; getting together with friends who share the experience and talking about what God might be teaching each of you; recording what you're thinking in a special journal; writing a short story or news report of the event (this can help you focus on facts, characters involved, emotions, and so on); or just writing freely in your journal.

What about spiritual disciplines — can they help me find a sense of balance?

First, what are spiritual disciplines? They're practices or exercises that help you grow closer to God, deepen your relationship with Christ, and strengthen your desire to be more like Christ. So certainly, practicing spiritual disciplines can help you find a sense of balance in your life. In fact, maybe no other practice or tip or help is as important as the regular and frequent practice of spiritual disciplines as you seek balance.

Spiritual disciplines are like good habits, but they go beyond mere routine or rite. As Donald Whitney notes in *Spiritual Disciplines for the Christian Life*, "Just as there is little value in practicing the scales on a guitar or piano apart from the purpose of playing music, there is little value in practicing spiritual disciplines apart from the single purpose that unites them. That purpose is godliness. We are told in 1 Timothy 4:7 to discipline ourselves 'for the purpose of godliness.'"[3]

No other practice or tip or help is as important as the regular and frequent practice of spiritual disciplines as you seek balance.

Whitney describes ten spiritual disciplines and adds that there are still others identified in Scripture. Here are those that Whitney includes and brief descriptions of each.[4]

Bible Intake

If your true sense of balance in life is going to come from God, it only makes sense that you need to be filled with His clear and direct communication to you. You can accomplish that by practicing the discipline that Whitney describes as Bible Intake. This "intaking" of God's Word is divided into six categories: hearing, reading, studying, memorizing, meditating, and applying.

If you don't discipline yourself to *hear* God's Word, you'll only hear it accidentally, just when you feel like it, or perhaps never. Jesus said, "Blessed rather are those who hear the word of God and obey it" (Luke 11:28). God further promises His blessings if you *read* His Word: "Blessed is the one who reads the words of this prophecy" (Revelation 1:3). And beyond reading Scripture, if you *study* God's Word you'll discover the clarity and detail of God's plan. In addition, Scripture calls you to *memorize* God's Word: "I have hidden your word in my heart that I might not sin against you" (Psalm 119:11); to *meditate* on God's Word: "Whatever is true, whatever is right, whatever is pure, whatever is lovely, whatever is admirable—if anything is excellent or praiseworthy—think about such things" (Philippians 4:8); and to *apply* God's Word to your life: "Do not merely listen to the word, and so deceive yourselves. Do what it says" (James 1:22).

Prayer

In Section 2, you read about how prayer can play a role in feeling balanced. Why do you need to pray? Whitney says, "God has not only spoken clearly and powerfully to us through Christ and the Scriptures, he also has a very large ear continuously open to us. He will hear every prayer of his children, even when our prayers are weaker than a snowflake."[5] Again, as you seek true balance in your life from your relationship with God, His answers to your prayers will allow you to discover what His will is for you and to grow closer to Him.

When it comes to practicing the discipline of prayer, Whitney points out that God expects you to pray: "Devote yourselves to prayer, being watchful and thankful" (Colossians 4:2). While anyone can simply talk to God, practicing the discipline of prayer is how you learn to pray more effectively. The disciples asked Christ, "Lord, teach us to pray" (Luke 11:1). And you can expect that prayer will be answered: "Ask and it will be given to you; seek and you will find; knock and the door will be opened to you. For everyone who asks receives; he who seeks finds; and to him who knocks, the door will be opened" (Matthew 7:7-8).

Worship

This discipline is important as you seek balance, because it will serve two related purposes: (1) It will humble you as you realize that you don't deserve any glory and that on your own, you're not worthy of a personal relationship with God; and (2) it will help you place your adoration and praise at the feet of the Person who does deserve glory and honor.

Whitney defines the discipline of worship as focusing on and responding to God. It's as simple as what Thomas said to the resurrected Jesus: "My Lord and my God!"

(John 20:28). Whitney writes, "The more we focus on God, the more we understand and appreciate how worthy he is. As we understand and appreciate this, we can't help but respond to Him."[6] As Jesus said in John 4:23-24, we worship in spirit and in truth: "Yet a time is coming and has now come when the true worshipers will worship the Father in spirit and truth, for they are the kind of worshipers the Father seeks. God is spirit, and his worshipers must worship in spirit and in truth."

Evangelism

This discipline relates to balance in that it is more about reaching outside yourself than it is trying to control your own life by withdrawing. In fact, one danger of reaching outside yourself is that *you* can't control what happens. But *God* can and does as you take a step of faith to practice this discipline. The gift of life that God has given you is something you should love so much that you want to share it. It's something that should shine through you so that you can even share it without words. And it should be so attractive that others will want it simply because they see God's love shining through you.

Whitney says that evangelism is simply communicating the gospel. Like the other disciplines listed, evangelism is expected of you: "Therefore go and make disciples of all nations, baptizing them in the name of the Father and of the Son and of the Holy Spirit, and teaching them to obey everything I have commanded you. And surely I will be with you always, to the very end of the age" (Matthew 28:19-20). Evangelism is also empowered within you—by the Holy Spirit, the presence of God Himself: "You will receive power when the Holy Spirit comes on you; and you will be my witnesses in Jerusalem, and in all Judea and Samaria, and to the ends of the earth" (Acts 1:8). You need to practice this discipline, not to actually evangelize, for that's a natural outflow of a Christian life; rather you must discipline yourself to get into the *context* of evangelism—looking for evangelism opportunities instead of just waiting for them to happen.

Serving

As you read earlier, serving is related to balance in your life because it places your focus on others rather than yourself. Serving can help you get outside yourself and beyond your own selfish motives and attitudes. It can help you move past pain and suffering you've experienced, either as you counsel others through what you've learned by your trial, or as you simply gain a new perspective of what others need.

Whitney says that serving needs to be practiced as a spiritual discipline because it isn't always glamorous. He says, "Although Christ's summons to service is the most spiritually grand and noble way to live a life, it is typically as pedestrian as washing someone's feet . . . serving is as commonplace as the practical needs it meets."[7] It's another discipline that is commanded of you: "It is the LORD your God you must follow, and him you must revere. Keep his commands and obey him; serve him and hold fast to him" (Deuteronomy 13:4). You've been given spiritual gifts directly from God to use in service: "Each one should use whatever gift he has received to serve others, faithfully administering God's grace in its various forms" (1 Peter 4:10). Finally, service that we do when motivated by God is always valuable: "Always give yourself fully to the work of the Lord, because you know that your labor in the Lord is not in vain" (1 Corinthians 15:58).

Stewardship

This spiritual discipline directly relates to balance.

Practicing this discipline can bring you balance—directly from God—in the areas of finances and time.

Regarding time, Whitney notes that Jesus so perfectly ordered His moments and His days that at the end of His earthly life He was able to pray to the Father, "I have brought you glory on earth by completing the work you gave me to do" (John 17:4). You practice the discipline of stewardship with your time because once time is lost, it simply can't be regained: "As long as it is day, we must do the work of him who sent me. Night is coming, when no one can work" (John 9:4). When it comes to finances, Whitney says that the discipline of stewardship is important because "there is a very real sense in which our money represents *us*. Therefore, how we use it expresses who we are, what our priorities are, and what's in our heart. As we use our money and resources Christianly, we prove our growth in Christlikeness."[8]

Fasting

How can this discipline possibly relate to finding and seeking balance? The answer to this question might be easier than you realize! Fasting is more than abstaining from food; it's denying yourself anything you normally do for a period of time in order to focus on spiritual activity. Naturally, as you abstain from food or any other physical need, you're able to focus on what and how God wants to work in your life. What greater way than that to find a sense of balance?

Think about the things that cause stress in your life—many of them are related directly to time or money.

Whitney notes that the discipline of fasting is another expected discipline. In a number of places in the Gospels, Jesus said, "When you fast . . . " not "If you fast . . . " so He obviously expected His followers to fast. Fasting is also to be done for a purpose. For example, Acts 13:3 notes that "after they had fasted and prayed, they placed their hands on [Barnabas and Saul] and sent them off [on the very first missionary journey]." Of course, fasting can be practiced for many other purposes, such as to strengthen your prayers, to seek God's guidance, to express grief, to seek deliverance or protection, to express repentance, to minister to others' needs, and even more.

Silence and Solitude

Similar to fasting, these disciplines can help you gain balance by getting away from all of life's distractions and noises and instead focusing on exactly what God has for you, how He wants to work in your life as you serve and obey Him.

Whitney points out that when you practice the discipline of silence, you voluntarily and temporarily abstain from speaking to seek certain spiritual goals; when you practice solitude, you voluntarily and temporarily withdraw to privacy for spiritual purposes. He says, "Think of silence and solitude as complementary disciplines to fellowship. Without silence and solitude we're shallow. Without fellowship we're stagnant. Balance requires them all."[9]

Grabbing Some Silence

Look for moments of silence during each day when you can pause to listen to God's voice. Plan periods of fifteen minutes to an hour; retreat to a room alone and shut the door or sit alone in your car. Use the time to pray silently, to focus on a single passage of Scripture, or to ask God to speak to you.

Worship God during a moment of silence. You might be accustomed to worshiping with hymns, choruses, Scripture passages, and prayer. But spend silent time contemplating who God is and how much He deserves your adoration and praise. God doesn't require an external demonstration to know that you're truly worshiping Him.

Find a nearby place away from people where you can practice this discipline when your home or workplace doesn't allow it. Look for a quiet park, find a nearby lake or beach, or seek out a spot in the mountains.

Practice silence with other disciplines such as solitude or fasting. Alternate among different disciplines during an extended time alone—fast for a day and spend a portion of the day in silence, a portion in deep prayer, and a portion meditating on a passage of Scripture.

Plan a longer retreat to practice the discipline of silence. Some monasteries and abbeys rent rooms; other options include a hotel room; staying at home while the rest of your family is at school, work, or other activities; or getting out of your own element by asking a friend if you can use his or her home for a day or two.

Journaling

This discipline relates to balance because it's something that can be practiced every day, and you can simply record exactly how—through the events and circumstances and occasions of your life—God is working in you.

Whitney uses a beautiful phrase to describe why so many Christians like to journal: "Since each believer's journey down life's river involves bends and hazards previously unexplored by [him] on the way to the Celestial City, something about journaling this journey appeals to the adventuresome spirit of Christian growth."[10]

Unlike other disciplines mentioned here, journaling isn't commanded in Scripture, but it is modeled. Whitney points out that many Psalms are records of David's journey with God, and the book of Lamentations is a journal of Jeremiah's feelings about the fall of Jerusalem. A journal is simply a book where you record various things; as a discipline, you record the works and ways of God in your life. This might include daily events, personal relationships, insights into Scripture, and prayer requests. Whitney adds that a journal is a valuable place to chart progress in practicing other spiritual disciplines and to hold yourself accountable to goals you've set.

Learning

Oh, how this term relates to balance! Learning is what you take in as you learn more about God and grow deeper and closer in your relationship to Him; a balanced life is the outward evidence and demonstration of all that you've taken in.

> ### Changed from the Inside Out
>
> So here's what I want you to do, God helping you: take your everyday, ordinary life—your sleeping, eating, going-to-work, and walking-around life—and place it before God as an offering. Embracing what God does for you is the best thing you can do for him. Don't become so well-adjusted to your culture that you fit into it without even thinking. Instead, fix your attention on God. You'll be changed from the inside out. . . . Unlike the culture around you, always dragging you down to its level of maturity, God brings the best out of you, develops well-formed maturity in you.
>   —Romans 12:1-2, MSG

Whitney points out that the word *disciple* means "to be not only 'a follower' of Christ but also 'a learner.' To follow Christ and become more like him, we must engage in the spiritual discipline of learning."[11] Why learning? Because learning characterizes the wise person: "Instruct a wise man and he will be wiser still; teach a righteous man and he will add to his learning" (Proverbs 9:9). Learning also transforms you into being more like Christ: "Do not conform any longer to the pattern of this world, but be transformed by the renewing of your mind" (Romans 12:2).

Finally, as you practice these good habits, remember their purpose—what you might call Christian maturity. That includes helping you grow closer to God, deepening your relationship with Christ, and strengthening your desire to be more like Christ.

Balance in Your Life

That best portion of a good

man's life: his little, nameless, unremembered

acts of kindness and of love.

William Wordsworth

Seeking Balance in Your Own Life

Did you ever see the movie *Groundhog Day?* Yes, another comedy starring Bill Murray! In this movie, Murray plays Phil Conners, a weatherman who gets sent to Punxsutawny, Pennsylvania, to report on whether another Phil—the groundhog—sees his shadow. In this age-old tradition, if the groundhog sees his shadow, winter lasts another six weeks. If it's a cloudy day, there's no shadow and winter ends.

What the weather is going to be like is the least of the sarcastic Phil Conners' problems. He covers the event in his usual sardonic style. But when he wakes up in his cozy bed-and-breakfast room as the digital clock flips to 6:00 the "next" morning, somehow it's Groundhog Day again. Over and over, Phil wakes up, only to discover once again that it's . . . Groundhog Day.

At first it's jarring. Then Phil has fun with it, realizing that if tomorrow will just be today again, he can get away with just about anything, such as robbing an armored car, crashing a car into a building, and punching the local insurance salesman—an old high school classmate. Then when Phil realizes the cycle may never end, it's depressing. He tries to kill himself—driving off a cliff into a rock quarry, jumping off a building, dropping a toaster into his bath. Yet each time, he wakes up at 6:00 the next morning. Finally, Phil realizes that maybe he's reliving the day until "he gets it right." He decides to learn how to play the piano, he counsels a couple debating whether to go through with their wedding, he saves a man who is choking—all because he knows from having lived through that day already exactly what's going to happen.

The real turning point seems to come when Phil tries to save a homeless man's life. For several days (that are actually the same day) Phil valiantly attempts different rescues. But each time, the man dies. Phil seems to learn something of the value of life through this—and the value of living and enjoying each day with the people around you. For the purposes of this book, let's just say that Phil finds a little bit of balance in his life.

Well, not to overspiritualize a little comedic romp—but what would you do if you could live the same day over and over? Or what would you do if you were forced to? Would you have fun with it? Would you take advantage of it in a negative way because you wouldn't face any consequences from your actions? Would it depress you to be stuck? Or would you learn something valuable from it?

In addition to the many spiritual imperatives you can follow to find balance, you can also do many practical things.

Of course, you won't get that chance. That's good and bad. If you relived the same day again and again, you might "finally get it right." But what if the particular day you were stuck with was a bad day? The good thing is that because you're a follower of Christ, you know that God's mercies are new every morning. No matter what you experienced yesterday, a week ago, years ago, or even as a child, God invites you to experience today anew with Him! And no matter what any of those past days looked like, He promises you His peace—a peace that passes all understanding. That's what balanced living is all about.

We've now explored what living a balanced life might look like (as well as what it isn't), we've examined what Scripture says about balance, and we've touched on areas that might help you find balance. But just how do you seek balance in your own life? While previous sections contain a few ideas for application, they focus more on figuring out what balance looks like. This section gets down to business. While you may see some of the same topics covered that you did in earlier sections, here you'll find many more practical ideas about *how* to use these areas to strengthen your sense of balance.

How can I prioritize my life in order to find balance?

As you've read many times along this journey to find balance, true balance can come only from God—from your personal relationship with God through His Son, Jesus Christ. But that doesn't mean that you're exempt from putting your own life in a place where God can work in it. God can't direct your life in the direction He desires if you're at a standstill—remember the old saying, "You can't steer a parked car?" Get moving so God can guide you.

In addition to the many spiritual imperatives you can follow to find balance, you can also do many practical things. Setting priorities in your life is one place to start.

Prioritizing can help bring balance to your life by helping you analyze whether a task or responsibility needs to be accomplished immediately or if it can wait. You can also think about whether to break a task down into a number of steps or if you want to (or need to) accomplish it all at once.

One way to think about how to prioritize all the things you need to accomplish is to list them in various categories. You can either do this mentally, on a notepad, or in some sort of planner where you keep a to-do list. The actual act of writing out these tasks usually provides some relief from the stress of trying to remember everything. That alone brings a measure of balance into your life.

There are a number of ways to set priorities. Here's one way that has worked for others. Try listing all of the tasks you need to accomplish in four quadrants as follows:

Importance: High *Urgency: High* **1**	Importance: High *Urgency: Low* **3**
Importance: Low *Urgency: High* **2**	Importance: Low *Urgency: Low* **4**

Now, simply categorize each of your tasks into one of the quadrants. If something seems unimportant right now and you have a long time to accomplish it, then it can be placed in quadrant 4. Something else may not seem important to you, but it has a short deadline—it can be listed in quadrant 2. If something does seem important, but you have a long time to get it done, list it in quadrant 3. Finally, if a task is both important and urgent, place it in quadrant 1.

The left side of the chart (quadrants 1 and 2) now becomes the list of tasks that you need to get to immediately. The right side (quadrants 3 and 4) are those tasks that can wait. Another way to think of this is that quadrant 1 is the "front burner." The tasks here are hot, in that you strongly desire to see them completed and you have a short time frame to accomplish them. Quadrant 4, on the other hand, is very much the "back burner." These tasks are not important to you at present and they either have no timetable or the deadline is so distant that you sense no urgency about getting them done.

Now that you've listed your priorities in this way, you can spend time working on all four quadrants. Again, you'll need to tackle 1 and 2 first, simply because deadlines are looming. You might try working on the tasks in quadrant 2 immediately; assigning them "low" importance is probably an indication that you don't particularly want to work on them. But if you complete these tasks first, working on the tasks in quadrant 1 will be more enjoyable. In free time, spare moments, work on the tasks on the right side of the chart. Again, working on those in 4 before tackling the tasks in 3 will help you enjoy working on the tasks that you've qualified as important.

Think of this chart as fluid. If you don't get to tasks in sections 3 and 4, they may need to move across the chart to sections 1 or 2.

Again, there are other ways to prioritize the tasks and routines of your life. You can divide them into areas of life: work, home, church, family, and so on. Or you can think of how you spend a typical day, and list your tasks on daily planner pages to create some habits and routine.

When you move beyond creating a list of tasks, prioritizing life can become more difficult. Dr. Richard Swenson, in his best-selling book *Margin,* points out that trying to arrange priorities probably won't work. He points out that we love God, spouse, children, self, and church all at the same time and all at a hundred percent. So it's impossible to prioritize them. He suggests instead thinking of God as central to all things and then building outward from that center point.[1]

While Dr. Swenson's advice is invaluable, the idea of prioritizing at least the tasks of your life is something practical—a way you can get your arms around the things that consume much of your life. Most important, the idea of finding balance through setting priorities comes from freeing your mind of agonizing over the list of things you need to accomplish, as well as creating a plan for how to organize and complete the tasks. And of course, you need to take the action to work on completing the tasks.

Summary

- Prioritize by determining if tasks are urgent.
- Determine also if tasks are important.
- Work first on tasks that are most urgent and important.
- Spend free time on tasks that have longer deadlines or that are less desirable.
- Feel balance by creating a plan of attack for setting priorities.
- This concept works better for prioritizing tasks; use extreme caution when prioritizing relationships.
- Setting priorities allows you to free your mind by creating a plan of attack for accomplishing the tasks of life.

Is it okay to say no sometimes?
What if I want to say no to a good cause?

Some people have absolutely no difficulty saying no to things. But maybe you're one of those people who can't say no. As a result, you might feel like the people around you take advantage of you.

Of course, not everyone who asks you to do something is trying to take advantage of you. The point is that you do need to be aware of and guard against those circumstances. You'll easily recognize when you're being taken advantage of if the same person constantly makes requests of you in order to get himself or herself out of a bind. Then you might need to learn to say no so that you're not enabling that person to be irresponsible.

If you're certain you're *not* in this kind of situation, then you can more reasonably and rationally decide to say "no" to reasonable and rational requests. One way to look for balance in this situation is to make sure you take enough time before you answer a request to truly contemplate what your answer should be. There may be a few worthy things in life that you can say no to immediately. But many people in the sales business will tell you that their profession is built on getting customers to say yes without taking the time to think about it. For example, if someone who sells cars hears you say, "It's such a big decision that I'd like to sleep on it," you'll probably hear back something to the effect of, "That's fine, but we might not be able to make you this same great deal tomorrow."

While not every immediate decision is necessarily a bad decision, you're much more likely to make good decisions if you think through all the ramifications. So, don't be afraid to practice and use that response of "I'll think about it and get back to you tomorrow." Then stick to your guns.

Other Voices

I think we have to learn to say no when we know we should. We need to learn to set boundaries for ourselves and our families to protect us from being over-committed. Good ideas aren't necessarily God's ideas.

—Laura

Decide ahead of time that you absolutely will not make a snap decision; if something's truly a good deal, it will still be there tomorrow. Or another deal—not necessarily better or worse—will be right behind it. Practicing this response and then using it relieves you of the pressure to respond immediately. Then, while alone, you can list all the pros and cons of saying yes or no.

Decide ahead of time that you absolutely will not make a snap decision.

An example might help here. Say someone asks you to serve on the worship committee at your church. He tells you all the reasons you should say yes: "You love God, don't you? Don't you want to serve Him? You appreciate good worship, right?" And then he builds you up: "You have great biblical insights about worshiping God. You're sensitive to what other people in the church want because you're a good listener. And you're good at confronting others when they're wrong about things." Well, how could you say no to such a sales job?

If this person seems to be sincere, instead of saying no, try to say something such as, "I need to think and pray about it—it sounds like a lot of responsibility and I want to make sure I'm serving in the right area. I'll get back to you a week from today with an answer."

Then away, on your own, make a list of pros and cons for yourself. For example, church committees are notorious for taking something people love and enjoy and turning that very thing into a chore. You may love worshiping God. But what if, as part of this committee, you have to be responsible for tough decisions about the style of worship your church uses? Or what if you end up in the position of needing to recommend firing a worship pastor?

> **Just Say No**
>
> Saying no can be the ultimate self-care.
>
> —Claudia Black

Other Voices

Know when to say no. What you're being asked to do may be a good and godly thing. But it may not be the right thing to do if it conflicts with your family or your own priorities. Filling your plate too full of good things isn't always better; sometimes it's just more.

— Lisa

Suddenly, worship isn't such a love and joy any more!

On the other hand, if you are dissatisfied with how your church approaches worship, and you feel strongly enough that you're prepared for the battle to make appropriate changes, then this may be the assignment for you.

The point is, no matter what you're being asked to do—or for that matter, buy or commit to in any way—don't hesitate to ponder your answer outside of the heat of the moment. And yes, you may end up saying no to something that's a very worthy cause or project. In this situation, you might soften your "no" answer by saying that you'll pray that the committee's leaders will find just the right person to fill the slot. In a work situation, you might suggest others who are better equipped to handle a responsibility you've decided to turn down. For salespeople, you might suggest that they contact you in six months or a year to see if your needs or financial situation have changed (but not if you really aren't interested in the product—you'll just have to go through the sales pitch again and muster the courage to say no again!).

Summary

- Guard against saying yes in any situation where it allows others to avoid their responsibilities—that's called enabling.
- Don't be afraid to delay your decision until a time when you can pray about it, ponder all your options, and think through the consequences of saying yes.

- While away from the heat of the situation, list the pros and cons of each side of the discussion you're facing. Don't forget to include how you feel—that's just as valid as the factual information.
- It's okay to say no. And it's okay to be tactful with your response. Just guard against leaving the door open for future pressure if you know you'll simply say no again later.

How can I find balance in my work?

For many people, finding balance in work is less of a problem than finding balance between work and all the other demands of life. Working forty hours a week at nearly any job simply consumes a large chunk of waking hours. It only takes simple math to see how work can overtake every other area of life. You might remember reading about this in the Introduction. Here's another way to look at what happens to a whole week—just where does it go?

Everyone's week begins with just 168 hours. Subtract forty-eight of that for sleeping, and you're down to 120. Now take away another forty-five minutes for each meal or about sixteen hours a week, and you're left with 104 hours. What about church commitments? Down to about 100 hours. Commuting time to work? Down to ninety-five. Finally, subtract the forty hours of work (which for many people becomes fifty or more), and there are only forty-five hours left in the week. Sound like a lot? You also have to prepare meals, do the laundry, take care of the lawn, have maintenance done on both cars, help kids with homework . . . you get the idea.

The fact is that for most of us, just our scheduled work hours consume more of our time than any other single activity, and that doesn't count working overtime, commuting, getting ready for work, or even just thinking about the work piled up on your desk (or wherever)! Remembering this is crucial when thinking about finding balance in the rest of your life, because you may not have as much time for other things as you think you do.

A Worker's Prayer

When lawyer Martin Camp realized after many years that he needed to stop shutting God out of his work life, he wrote a prayer for workers. As you seek to find balance in your work, you might want to pray it or adapt its concepts for yourself:

God, be with me this day in all of my life. Do not let me shut you out of any part. I need you in my work as well as in my personal life. I need to turn to you in praise as well as in sorrow, in joy as well as in sadness.

I need you in my marriage and all of my relationships. I need you in my inner struggles, too. In the depths of my soul, I cry out for help, for forgiveness, and for renewal.

Help me to accept both life's blessings and life's struggles, neither boasting nor complaining. Free me from the slavery of seeking the approval of others. Let me live simply and completely, with a forgiving heart and an open mind.

Lord, help me learn to listen—to you, to my [spouse], to my children, to my friends, to my colleagues. Grant me patience, compassion, and perseverance. Teach me to accept and love myself, so that I can love others.

My job requires much effort, and I need your guidance. Keep me productive and free from doubt and worry. Help me to do a good day's work, and then leave it behind. Help me find time for all that must be done, a discerning mind and heart to accomplish what can be done, and to accept what cannot be accomplished in this twenty-four-hour day.

Most of all, give me the joy for life that comes only from the movement of the Holy Spirit in my life. Lift me up and sustain me with your love, and at the end of this day, grant me peace and a carefree mind, secure in the knowledge of your love. Amen.[2]

If you're a workaholic—someone who is actually addicted to work—the idea of finding balance in this area of life is even more complex. As a workaholic, your work supercedes nearly all the other demands in your life, including your relationships with spouse, family, friends, and even God.

While this kind of complete and total commitment to work was once thought of as admirable, even employers are now realizing that it can actually be unhealthy. As Brian Robinson, author of *Chained to the Desk* notes, "The data says . . . that workaholics are not as efficient as non-workaholics. They tend to be hard to get along with. They often affect the morale of the company because they are moving so fast that they make a lot of mistakes. They are pushing other people. They are a risk for burnout and physical problems."[3]

Think you might be a workaholic? Psychologist Laura Struhl notes these warning signs of workaholism:

- Your home is just another office.
- You are hard driving, competitive, and overly committed to your work.
- You take office equipment with you wherever you go, even on vacations.
- Work makes you happier than other things in life.
- Sleep and recreational time seem like a waste to you.
- You get restless on vacations (if you take them) and sometimes cut them short.
- You frequently problem-solve work situations, even during your time off.
- If your friends still bother to call you, you can't wait to get them off the phone and return to work.
- You're tired, irritable, socially isolated, and might even have physical stress symptoms that include headaches, insomnia, shortness of breath, racing heart, muscle tension, or ulcers.[4]

If you recognize yourself in this list, you're probably a workaholic. Another measurement is to gauge yourself against a survey of 800 senior-level executives surveyed by Exec-U-Net, an Internet-based career management center. Male executives who considered themselves workaholics worked an average of 59.9 hours a week; female workaholics said they worked 56.9 hours. Even executives who didn't perceive themselves to be workaholics averaged 55.4 hours a week. Hmmmm. For the sake of argument, let's just say to watch out if you consistently work more than 45 or 50 hours every week.[5]

Okay, so you admit it—you're a workaholic. What can you do about it? Struhl lists these suggestions:

Schedule time for your primary relationship. Spend at least twenty to thirty minutes of "connect time" every day, not including time to discuss bills, children, phone calls, and so on. Instead, make future plans, dream together, and enjoy each other's company.

Make time for other friendships. Pick other people who help you have fun; if necessary, schedule time for nurturing relationships on your calendar.

Take care of your body. Take care of the basics: eating, sleeping, exercising.

Other Voices

Never, never compromise what you believe for the sake of your job or approval of coworkers. It will come back to bite you every time. Instead, be transparent about who you are and what's important to you. Otherwise, you'll constantly be trying to find one balance at work and another in the rest of your life. This never works. It's counterproductive and it won't take long for the people you work with to see right through you. And instead of respecting you for living up to your ideas, they'll think of you as a fraud.

—Robert

Reexamine your long-term goals. From the vantage point of your deathbed, what do you hope to say about how you've spent your career years?

Reexamine your short-term goals. Daily, remind yourself of what you've already accomplished, instead of dwelling only on what you still need to get done. A moment of reflection can help you keep things in perspective.

Consider counseling. Following someone else's instructions can be tough, but try it for at least a month before going back to your old ways.[6]

Maybe you're not a workaholic. Maybe for you, work just gets out of hand occasionally. You can usually leave work at work, or your job doesn't allow you to bring tasks home. Even if this describes you better, you need to keep work itself in balance when you're in the midst of it. Here are some practical suggestions:

- If possible, take breaks when you're supposed to. If you work at a job where you determine your own breaks and lunch times, make sure to get away from your desk. If you're not hungry, at least go for a walk around the block or around the building.

- No matter what level you're at in your company or organization, try to think of everyone else's work as just as important as your own. This will help when you're in meetings about who should take on new tasks, or even just in informal conversation at the coffeemaker when you find yourself grumbling about your workload.

Be sure you focus on renewing yourself physically, mentally, emotionally, and spiritually.

- Unless you have evidence that other employees aren't fulfilling their responsibilities, try not to compare what you're doing with what others around you are accomplishing. You may have busy days when others have slow days and vice versa.

- As in most relationships, try to listen to others twice as much as you speak. The old saying that "God gave you two ears and one mouth for a reason" holds a lot of truth in most work situations. Coworkers easily tire of know-it-alls, complainers, and sarcastic grumps. Try not to be one.

- When you listen to others at work, really listen. Don't be thinking of what you want to say next. Instead, allow for lulls in conversation so you can ponder what others say. "Reflect" back what someone else says: "What I'm hearing you say is . . ." is a good way to start that reflection.

- If you have a lot of tasks to accomplish each day, use the prioritizing system in the previous question to help organize your workload. Again, committing these tasks to paper often helps lessen their burden. Also, consider dividing your day into blocks of time. If you're most productive in the morning, use that time to tackle your toughest tasks. Spend the down time of the early afternoon to return phone calls, draft correspondence, and answer e-mails.
- Keep God in your work. As you've read earlier, even in the most boring or undesirable work, God calls you to work as if you're working for Him.
- Use your vacation. Don't end the year with your boss or some human relations rep saying, "If you don't use this vacation time by December 31, you'll lose it." Be sure to really take time off for holidays, vacations, and the like.
- If you're sick, arrange to stay home to recover. For most people, a day or two of recovery gets them back on track much faster than limping along at half capacity in their jobs for several weeks. Of course, don't abuse this privilege either.
- Arrange for a personal retreat. This can be as simple as spending a day reading your Bible at a local park, or a more elaborate and lengthy time away in a lodge, hotel room, or monastery. During your retreat, be sure you focus on renewing yourself physically, mentally, emotionally, and spiritually. In other words, don't bring along half the office with you.

20 Ideas for Stress Relief at Work

1. Define realistic expectations of what you can and can't do.
2. Maintain a strong support network of family and friends.
3. Establish realistic and reachable goals.

4. Retrace your steps to the period before you began to feel stressed; how can you reestablish priorities if you could go back to that point?

5. Change your eating habits—get nutritious.

6. Exercise more—take a walk at lunch.

7. Set aside a time each day to pray about your stress, surrendering it to God.

8. Reduce your workload—you don't have to do everything yourself.

9. Learn to say no when you're asked to do more than you can.

10. Pace yourself—balance work with other areas of life.

11. Rediscover your sense of humor.

12. Renew relationships with people who make you feel at ease.

13. Talk about your feelings—don't keep anger or frustration inside.

14. Change your circumstances—take a day off, go on a vacation, or begin searching for a new job if necessary.

15. Manage your time—do some important things along with some of the urgent. Even do a few things you want and like to do.

16. Get some extra sleep—discover the art of napping or turn in an hour earlier each night.

17. Renew your vision: "Where there is no vision, the people perish." (Proverbs 29:18, KJV)

18. Don't deny your feelings—ask God to help you with what you're going through.

19. Get a checkup—maybe the stress is being aggravated by something physical.

20. Don't stress about stress. Ask friends to help you evaluate if you're "making a mountain out of a molehill."

How can I find balance in my leisure time?

Like work, leisure time can be more a matter of balancing it as a whole against the other demands of your time. Again, the average American spends seven hours sleeping, seven-and-a-half hours working, one hour and eighteen minutes commuting, one-and-a-half hours eating, and six-and-a-half hours watching television, leaving just forty-two minutes of other leisure time![7]

Want to think of this in even more shocking terms? Look at how the average person spends his time in a year:

- the equivalent of 106 days sleeping
- the equivalent of 114 days working
- nearly twenty days commuting
- nearly twenty-three days eating (we're pigs!)
- almost 100 days watching television

Before you declare that you're not average, think about your own day. Maybe you don't watch nearly this much TV, but do you spend time surfing the Web or writing and answering personal e-mails? What about driving children and yourself to appointments, sports events, music lessons, and so on? Or do you spend several hours a week shopping for groceries, clothing, and other family needs? It's easy to eat up a considerable amount of time even if you aren't the stereotypical couch potato.

So as you seek balance in leisure time, the first step is making sure that you *have* leisure time. God worked for six days and rested one. Do you set aside at least one-seventh of your time for rest and recreation?

Measure yourself against this using those average American numbers: There are 10,080 minutes in each seven-day week. One-seventh of that time is 1,440 minutes. If you sleep seven-and-a-half

> **On Guard!**
>
> Keep a cool head. Stay alert. The Devil is poised to pounce, and would like nothing better than to catch you napping. Keep your guard up.
> —1 Peter 5:8-9, MSG

hours each night, that consumes 450 of those minutes. But that still leaves 990 minutes per week of time you should be resting and relaxing and recreating. That's over 140 minutes per day—two hours and twenty minutes. Considerably more than forty-two minutes!

I'm sure you could tear apart all of these mathematical gymnastics. What about vacations? What about long holiday weekends? Go ahead—do your own calculations. You'll still come to realize that you probably don't create enough leisure time for yourself.

Truth is, if you took two hours each day to do absolutely nothing, you'd probably go crazy. That's a reality of our culture. But are there fun and relaxing things you could do with a couple of hours a day? Some ideas:

Other Voices

Recreation shouldn't be the sole focus of life, but it's an important part of balanced living. It's a constant battle for me to slow down because I'm naturally a "multi-tasker," and I've always thought that I have to be doing something useful all the time. I had to learn that it's okay to spend a few hours "unplugged" without feeling guilty about what I'm not accomplishing.

—Lisa

- Learn a new craft or hobby.
- Read to your kids.
- Swing in a porch swing or hammock.
- Spend more time studying the Bible or in a daily quiet time.
- Grab a twenty-minute nap each day.
- Go walking or hiking.
- Roll in a pile of leaves with your children and spouse.
- Sip iced tea on the front porch or back deck.
- Go to a park or the beach.
- Sip coffee and leisurely browse in a bookstore.
- Hug each family member for a whole minute each day (with a lot of time left over).

You get the picture. Balance will come more easily in the whole of life when you make time for leisure time.

How can I be satisfied with my physical appearance?

You may be wondering what this question is doing in a book on balance. The truth is, some people become so concerned about what they look like that it dominates their thoughts. For example, an overweight person might constantly think about his weight—will I be able to buckle my seat belt if I ride to lunch with this coworker or take a business trip on an airplane? Are people talking about me and my weight behind my back? I run out of breath when I take the stairs at work, but will I set off the alarm if I ride the elevator?

Other people become concerned about how they dress. Still others worry about baldness, personal hygiene, hair color and style, and on this list could go.

The simple answer is that if something bothers you, work on it. If you're overweight, change your eating habits and get more exercise. Ask your physician, a trainer, or nutritionist to help if you don't have the willpower to tackle the problem yourself. If you want to dress with a certain look, hunt through the library for magazines and books to help you, or search on the Internet for ideas. If you can't afford a certain level of clothing, shop at thrift stores.

The same can be said of anything about your physical appearance that bothers you—work

Other Voices

My appearance affects my sense of balance when I compare myself to others and fall short of the mark. I struggled for years with the reason for my existence, feeling like I didn't deserve good things or like I was in the way. I sometimes believed that there was no purpose for my life except to make others unhappy with me. Then I learned to see myself as God sees me. I was created by His hand with a specific purpose. I was lovingly planned and formed by God and He has a special purpose that only I can fulfill. That was when I realized that I look the way I do because God determined it, not by accident. My appearance and existence became a blessing, not a curse, because of the wonderful perspective God can bring to life.

—Julie

to change it. If you don't like how you look wearing glasses, consider contact lenses. Get a new haircut that flatters your facial shape. Grow a beard or shave one off.

Also, work to accept some things about yourself. If you're forty, you may not want to set the goal of dressing like a teenager. If your hair is gray, instead of coloring it, claim Proverbs 16:31: "Gray hair is a crown of splendor; it is attained by a righteous life." Some things you may want to change for health reasons or just because you can; other things you may want to change your attitude about.

How can I be satisfied with my mind and mental capacities?

Like most areas of life where you're seeking balance, it might be better to think of your mind or mental health and attitude as one part of overall balance. Your mind is like the home page on an Internet site; if a web browser can't find a home page, he won't benefit from any of the information on the rest of the site, simply because it's much more difficult for the user to get there. The home page contains the hyperlinks to the rest of the site.

Your mind is similar. If you're not healthy

A Prepared Life

Oh yes, you shaped me first inside, then out; you formed me in my mother's womb.
I thank you, High God—
you're breathtaking! Body and soul, I am marvelously made!
I worship in adoration—
what a creation!
You know me inside and out, you know every bone in my body;
You know exactly how I was made, bit by bit, how I was sculpted from nothing into something.
Like an open book, you watched me grow from conception to birth; all the stages of my life were spread out before you,
The days of my life all prepared before I'd even lived one day.
—Psalm 139:13-16, MSG

mentally, your mind will be impaired in its ability to send out information to the rest of your body. If you don't consciously ponder how you can improve your health, for example, you may not start a new exercise program or eat nutritious foods. If you don't consciously consider how to manage your anger or stress, you can actually become physically ill. And this is to say nothing of the subconscious role the mind plays—as well as all the involuntary bodily functions it properly controls when it's healthy.

All this to say, it's wise to take care of your mind.

If you're not healthy mentally, your mind will be impaired in its ability to send out information to the rest of your body.

You might think of a three-step process of keeping yourself mentally healthy—building your mental muscle, freeing your mental memory banks of unnecessary and unwanted information, and filling your mind with healthy thoughts. While the following list isn't comprehensive or exhaustive, it can at least give you a good start toward staying healthy mentally. And it will allow you to be in tune with yourself if something is lacking that you can take care of.

Disclaimer: Like other areas of seeking balance, if you sense that you have serious mental health problems, seek professional counseling to get you through your deepest and darkest times.

The idea here is to treat your mind like a muscle and to exercise it regularly. If you don't do some valuable mental gymnastics on a consistent basis, your mind will atrophy. What tools you use to exercise are nearly as important as the exercise itself. You want to work out your mind with the best equipment you can get. As the old saying goes, "Garbage in, garbage out." You want to aim for the opposite: "Good stuff in, good stuff out."

Here are three steps you can follow in that good start toward mental healthiness.

1. Build your mind by:

Reading the newspaper every day. Whether it's *The New York Times* or your local newspaper, stay current with events of the world, nation, and your local area. Ask yourself some evaluative questions once you've read the news, such as, (1) Is there anything I've read that would help me personally or professionally? (2) Have I read something that seems unlikely or impossible to believe, something that may have been misreported or biased—and perhaps I should find out more from another source? (3) Are there people or groups here that I can pray for? Reading with these ideas in mind will take the news beyond information and help it be more of a tool that will give your mind a workout.

Reading a weekly news magazine. In fact, you may want to read more than one news magazine to check their biases against each other so that you compile a more complete and balanced perspective of reported events. Ask yourself similar questions as listed above to benefit the most from this exercise. If you can't afford subscriptions to newspapers or magazines, remember that your local library most certainly carries a number of periodicals, and many titles are also available on the World Wide Web.

Listening to the challenges of people around you and carefully considering them. As challenging as it might be to make time to keep up with the world's news, this concept may actually be a far more challenging mental exercise.

Reading for information and pleasure. Whether you like mysteries or biographies, how-to books or self-help books, give yourself permission to exercise this part of your brain too.

2. Free your mind by:

Asking God to remove impure thoughts. This is the first step in mental warfare. God may put new thoughts into your head. He may distract you with some work He needs you to do. Don't be afraid to call on Him because He already knows your mind anyway.

Admitting to God that you desire to sin. Because He knows your desires, ask Him to strengthen your mental resistance. Ask Him to place His desires in your heart as He's promised to do. Give Him permission to take the Scripture you've hidden in your heart and bring it to the forefront of your mind.

3. Fill your mind by:

Reading Scripture every day. Remember Psalm 119:9-11: "How can a young man keep his way pure? By living according to your word. I seek you with all my heart; do not let me stray from your commands. I

Creative Minds
Imagination is more important than knowledge.
—Albert Einstein

have hidden your word in my heart that I might not sin against you." Be diligent in studying God's Word with your mind so that it makes its way to the corners of your heart.

Asking God daily to fill your mind with pure images and positive thoughts. Maybe your brain has an endless capacity to store images and thoughts. But in case it doesn't, ask God to remove the vileness that's in there and replace it with images that help you dwell on His character.

Listening to God's answers to your daily times of prayer. It isn't that easy to do. It's much easier to fill your prayer time with your own words. But prayer should be a time for two-way communication. Just like you need to be quiet to hear another person speaking, you need to be still if you want to listen to God's voice.

How can I be satisfied with my money and possessions?

Just for fun, check out these brief quotes about money:
- The one book that always has a sad ending is a checkbook.

- Contentment is when your earning power equals or exceeds your yearning power.
- Debts are about the only thing you can acquire without money.
- Money not only changes hands—it changes people.
- If you overestimate the value of money, you'll never be happy by amassing more of it.
- It's so difficult to save money when your neighbors keep buying things you can't afford!
- Money is a good servant but a poor master.
- If money is all you want, money may be all you'll get.
- Money cannot buy one necessity of the soul.
- Money will do more *to* you than it will do *for* you.[8]

Financial Difficulty

There are three conversions necessary: the conversion of the heart, mind, and purse. Of hese three, the conversion of the purse is most difficult.

—Martin Luther

Probably no subject has been written about and discussed and analyzed and grieved over more than money. The Bible has a lot to say about money too; like it or not, money is also a spiritual topic. In fact, some people have called money and materialism Christianity's greatest competition.

Briefly, what does the Bible have to say about your finances, and what principles can you learn for finding balance with your money and possessions?

Matthew 6:19-21: "Do not store up for yourselves treasures on earth, where moth and rust destroy, and where thieves break in and steal. But store up for yourselves treasures in heaven, where moth and rust do not destroy, and where thieves do not break in and steal. For where your treasure is, there your heart will be also." While there's nothing inherently wrong with money or wealth, when it becomes more important in your life than your work for God, that's a reflection of where your heart is. To avoid facing this problem,

Jesus encourages you to focus on God's work. Then you won't have this conflict in your life.

Matthew 19:21-24: "Jesus answered, 'If you want to be perfect, go, sell your possessions and give to the poor, and you will have treasure in heaven. Then come, follow me.' When the young man heard this, he went away sad, because he had great wealth." The young man in this example had great wealth. Jesus wanted to know the level of his commitment to God. Obviously, his money was more important than his relationship with God, because he wasn't willing to give it up. If you want balance in the area of finances, you don't have to give up everything. But you need to be *willing* to.

> ## True Riches
>
> "Tell those rich in this world's wealth to quit being so full of themselves and so obsessed with money, which is here today and gone tomorrow. Tell them to go after God, who piles on all the riches we could ever manage—to do good, to be rich in helping others, to be extravagantly generous. If they do that, they'll build a treasury that will last, gaining life that is truly life."
> —1 Timothy 6:17-19, MSG

1 Corinthians 16:2: "On the first day of every week, each one of you should set aside a sum of money in keeping with his income, saving it up, so that when I come no collections will have to be made." A proper attitude about giving will demonstrate itself if you're serious about your commitment to God. Your giving will be both systematic ("on the first day of every week") and generous ("in keeping with his income").

Philippians 4:19: "My God will meet all your needs according to his glorious riches in Christ Jesus." Balance in life comes from realizing that everything belongs to God to begin with. He meets all your needs because all the riches are His. You only give back to Him a portion of what He gives to you.

Taking Control of Money Matters

Not knowing where you are financially can cause you to lie awake at night. Use this checklist to ease your stress about finances by taking stock of where you are. While everything you have comes from God and still belongs to Him, He's charged you with stewardship over your finances (see Luke 16). That means not worrying about money because God will provide for your needs. But it also means that God expects you to make financial plans and to invest wisely.

Gather the following documents, determine if you have any gaps in your financial portfolio, and then make plans as a good steward of what God has provided.

General financial records. Gather together your tax returns; wills and trust documents; pay stubs for your current job; and statements for checking and savings accounts, bank CDs, mutual funds, brokerage accounts, and credit card accounts.

Insurance policies. Locate or obtain copies of life, disability, renter/homeowner, umbrella, medical/dental, automobile policies.

Real estate documents. Gather titles/ownership records, original prices of your house/condo, mortgage, home-equity loans.

Retirement plans. Pull together documentation of 401(k)/403(b) plans, IRAs, Keogh accounts.

Records of employee benefits. Collect documents pertaining to cafeteria plans, stock options, health and other insurance benefits, bonuses.

Valuables. Create a list of appraisals for collectibles, antiques, artwork, jewelry, and other valuables you own.

How can I manage my time better?

You've already read quite a bit about how easily time slips away. You've read about how the average person spends his or her time.

Imbalance and discontentment about time and its use often come from feeling that you simply don't have enough of it. While time management alone can't miraculously give a feeling of balance, not letting your time control you will certainly put you in a much better place to sense balance and contentment in life.

If you want to regain control of your time, here are a few steps you can take:

Take time off. Pick at least one day of the week where you will do no work related to your employment or any work or business you've got going on the side (your Internet business or your part-time job at the coffee shop). Choose any day that allows you to stay completely away from work. Turn on the answering machine, turn off your cell phone, and allow yourself to vegetate. Don't go to your workplace, don't check business e-mail, don't open your briefcase! Load up the car and take a day trip on the road, if necessary.

Block out time for yourself and your family. If you have school children, sit down with your spouse at the beginning of each school quarter or semester and record important dates—such as school programs and athletic events—into your calendar. Once a month, review those dates and enter any new ones. Then block out time to "date" your spouse and each of your children. You might also plan a night each week for a family activity—rent a movie together, go mini-golfing, eat at a favorite restaurant, or just go for a long drive together. If someone at work or church wants to schedule an appointment or meeting during any of these times, you can simply check

---

Other Voices

Balance isn't about time management; it's about life management. It isn't about preventing times of turmoil and panic; it's about having a way to reestablish equilibrium when the crisis has passed.

—Tim

your calendar and say that you're already booked! You certainly don't need to defend the importance of your marriage and family relationships.

Schedule time for ministry or service opportunities. If you're already involved in church or community service, that's great. Now be sure that you're leaving enough time in your schedule to accomplish your responsibilities with excellence. Don't dump on others that you serve or volunteer with. If your time is limited, see if your employer can arrange for you to do community service as part of your workday, or if that's not an option, consider doing volunteer or church service as a family. Make sure it's an activity that everyone enjoys at least one thing about.

> ## Where Do You Light the Candle?
>
> I've learned that balance does not mean we are good at everything. It means we do what we do well and get help with the rest. It means we do not make the mistake of lighting the candle at both ends and putting a match to the middle.
>
> —Liz Curtis Higgs[9]

If you have the flexibility in your job, divide your days into blocks. Think of your active days as having three main sections: breakfast to lunch, lunch to dinner, and dinner to bedtime. Now, try to schedule only two of these three blocks each day so that you have down time in at least one of the blocks. If that's not possible, determine to give yourself three or four "blocks" off per week in addition to your full day off. If you have church and school activities three nights per week, don't fill up the other nights with more activities. Or if you work an odd schedule, don't simply fill up your entire day with extracurricular activities.

Take a personal retreat day. Set your own goal of one day per month, per quarter, or per year. You know yourself and your schedule best. The idea of an occasional retreat is to escape the regular grind so that when you return to it you'll have a fresh perspective. If the idea of a retreat seems like too much of a luxury, alternate working retreats (getting away from the office for a day to complete—or start—that huge project you've been putting off); prayer retreats (spending a day at a park or in a hotel room just talking to and listening to God); and pure peaceful escapes (reading a novel in the backyard sun, sitting on a quiet beach, or hiking in the mountains).

How can I find balance in my relationships with members of my family?

Let's look briefly at what Scripture has to say about relationships with various family members.

Parents and Children

Ephesians 6:1-2 says, "Children, obey your parents in the Lord, for this is right. 'Honor your father and mother'—which is the first commandment with a promise—'that it may go well with you and that you may enjoy long life on earth.'"

> Your goal is not just children who obey you "because you say so." Your goal is children who obey you because they love you.

How does this verse relate to seeking balance in your relationship with your parents? As an adult child, you should recognize and acknowledge that if your parents taught you discipline and as you obeyed them out of your love for them, you're now enjoying the fruits of that relationship. You've learned self-discipline; because of their work as parents, you enjoy a relatively stable life. If you didn't have parents who did this, you can still honor them by forgiving them; that can also bring a sense of stability and balance to your life.

How does it affect seeking balance in your relationship with your children? As a parent, you want to foster the kind of relationship described above. You want to follow the advice of the often-quoted Proverbs 22:6: "Train a child in the way he should go, and when he is old he will not turn from it." Your instruction and discipline should follow the pattern of God, the heavenly Father—your goal is not just children who obey you "because you say so." Your goal is children who obey you because they love you; the result is adult children who love God, have a healthy personal relationship with Him, who know discernment and self-discipline, and who have relatively stable lives.

Spouse

Ephesians 5:22-28 instructs, "Wives, submit to your husbands as to the Lord. For the husband is the head of the wife as Christ is the head of the church, his body, of which he is the Savior. Now as the church submits to Christ, so also wives should submit to their husbands in everything. Husbands, love your wives, just as Christ loved the church . . . husbands ought to love their wives as their own bodies. He who loves his wife loves himself."

How does this relate to finding balance in your marriage? What the Bible says about marriage in this passage has been misinterpreted and abused by people ranging from feminists to spousal abusers. But the hallmark of the marriage relationship is *agape* love—a love that seeks the highest good for another person. It's the kind of love Christ demonstrated when He died on the cross.

The picture here is one of Christ's relationship with the church—Christ being the husband and the church (all believers) being His bride. While Christ is the head of the church, with total authority over it, He never abuses that position. He so loves the church that He always wants the best for it. He loves the church so much that He even died for it. This passage is

> ## Total Surrender
>
> Only when men and women give themselves to each other in total surrender, that is, with their whole person for their whole life, can their encounter bear full fruits.
>
> —Henri Nouwen

saying that if you're a wife, you will love your husband—and not try to take away his authority—because you know that he would go so far as to die for you to demonstrate his love for you. And if you're a husband, you have the responsibility to show your wife that you love her so much you would even die for her. And just as Christ would never abuse His authority over the church because He loves it too much, you would never abuse your authority over your wife. In fact, because of your love for her, you'll likely elevate her to a partnership, as Christ has done with the church.

Balance can occur within this unique and miraculous partnership and bond of a Christian marriage: "For this reason a man will . . . be united to his wife, and the two will become *one flesh*" (Ephesians 5:31, emphasis added). Perhaps because the bond between a husband and wife is deeper and more sacred than any other relationship on earth, husbands and wives will be able to see when life is out of balance for the other. Therefore, the marks of a good friendship (see the next question) should be even clearer in a marriage relationship. Likewise, husbands and wives will give each other permission to hold the other accountable. (See **I've heard a lot about accountability. Do I need a friend or group to help me seek balance?** on page 111.) In fact, because this relationship is patterned after the relationship Christ has with the church, it should embody and reflect all of the characteristics of balance outlined in this book.

How can I find balance in my friendships?

Why do you need a friend? You need someone who can celebrate with you or cry with you. You need someone who will give you comfort when you're in the pits, and someone who laughs with you during life's highs.

Good friends will listen to you at least as much as they talk about themselves. Good friends won't try to top your stories with their own.

You need someone in the day-to-day uneventful events of life. You need someone you can always count on. These kinds of friendships might be your most valuable possessions. And they certainly can help bring a sense of balance to your life as you go through the common "give and take" of friendships.

As you look for an earthly friend, Jesus offers you an unbelievable relationship as a friend.

What does that mean? Here are some qualities that mark true friendships. Notice how friendship is always a two-way street—what you expect from the relationship you must be willing to give.

True friends are honest with each other. As a good friend, you'll lovingly tell your friends when you see problems or mistakes or bad decisions; and you'll listen when your friends observe these traits in you. As a good friend you'll take the risk to point out in loving honesty the things that diminish your friends; you'll listen and accept when friends point out these things to you.

True friends are good listeners. If your friends only want to talk about their own problems, their own interests, their own lives—you might want to evaluate if those friendships are authentic. Good friends will listen to you at least as much as they talk about themselves. Good friends won't try to top your stories with their own. When you hear the words "Hey, you think that's bad, you should have seen the time I . . . " it might be time to look for different friends. If you catch yourself saying something like this, it might be time to start listening more and talking less before your friends move on to a new and improved version of a friend. As a good friend, you'll listen to your friends; you'll sincerely desire to know how the other person feels; you'll want to know what concerns him or her.

True friends protect their relationship with each other. What does that look like? Good friends will keep your private conversations private. They won't gossip about the things you've shared with them, and you'll keep the things they tell you in confidence. You and your friends will commit to pray for one another. Your true friends won't allow other people to speak poorly of you, and you'll do the same for them.

True friends bear each other's burdens: "A friend loves at all times, and a brother is born for adversity" (Proverbs 17:17). It's easy to be a friend when times are good, when there's plenty of fun to share, plenty of wealth to throw around. But a true friend will be there for you when times aren't so good—if you lose your job, if you're suffering from poor health, if someone close to you dies, or if you're just plain down in the dumps. And, of course, you'll be there in the same way when your friends are down too.

So, where do you find a friend like this? You're ready! You can commit to these qualities! You know you can hold up your end of the bargain if you can just find one other person to do the same.

True friendships can take years to develop to this level. But the starting point is to ask God to provide a friend who can become these things for you—and to whom you can offer these same qualities. Then look around. Is there someone in your church who seems to embody these qualities and who shares some common interests with you? Is there a friend from a past stage of life—high school, college, a past job—who you can look up again? Is there a family member who can also be a true friend? Or has God put your spouse into your life to become this kind of friend?

Whenever and wherever you find a potential friend, begin a simple relationship. A sure way to kill a friendship before it even starts is by proclaiming, "I really need a good friend to lean on." Instead, just spend some time together doing things you both like to do. Take the time to discover if your personalities rub each other the wrong way, or if your discussions rub more like Proverbs 27:17: "As iron sharpens iron, so one man sharpens another."

Finally, don't forget that as you look for an earthly friend, Jesus offers you an unbelievable relationship as a friend. Jesus said, "I no longer call you servants, because a servant does not know his master's business. Instead, I have called you friends, for everything that I learned from my Father I have made known to you" (John 15:15). Whether or not you develop a close relationship with a fellow Christian on earth, as a follower of Christ, you need and already have the wonderful friendship of Christ. This is still a mutual friendship—if you'll allow Him to, He'll reveal God's big-picture plan to you and He'll use you to help fulfill that plan. And at the same time, you can confide everything in Jesus and know that He won't reject you. He knows you better than you know yourself (Matthew 10:30). He promises that He will *never* leave you nor forsake you (Hebrews 13:5). His very own blood blots out your sins (Hebrews 9:14)! Who could ask for a better friend?

Balance in the Everyday

Relying on God has to begin

all over again every day as if nothing yet had

been done.

C. S. Lewis

Living Out Balance Every Day

The movie *Liar, Liar!* stars Jim Carrey as Fletcher Reed, a ruthless lawyer who can sell his services to any client and talk his way to victory in any courtroom. But one person can still melt his heart—his son, Max. Unfortunately, Fletcher even stretches the truth when it comes to his relationship with Max. He lies to Max when he can't keep his commitments; worse, he misleads himself about just how good his parenting relationship is with his son.

But even Max knows his dad shouldn't lie. So when Fletcher misses Max's birthday party, the son makes an unusual wish—that his dad can't tell a lie for "just one day." When Max's wish comes true, Fletcher's sweet-talking, fast-talking mouth becomes his biggest liability.

Is balance in life something you can find in "just one day"? No, but a day may be a good place to start. If after all of this reading, and after your own prayers and study, you're still struggling with finding contentment and balance in life, maybe you need to break it down into a daily skirmish, rather than a huge world war. You might find your battle cry in Lamentations 3:22-23:

Nothing Slips Through

God's love is meteoric,
his loyalty astronomic,
His purpose titanic,
his verdicts oceanic.
Yet in his largeness
nothing gets lost;
Not a man, not a mouse,
slips through the cracks.
—Psalm 36:5-6, MSG

Because of the LORD'S great love we are not consumed,
for his compassions never fail.
They are new every morning;
great is your faithfulness.

How awesome! God's mercy, His compassion, is new every day. Each day He will do everything He has faithfully promised to do. Each day is a new day, a new gift from God.

That means that you can fight the skirmish for balance today, and let tomorrow, next week, and next year go (as well as yesterday, last week, and last year). To help you with that daily skirmish, let's review some of the concepts from your earlier reading. Here's a top ten list for finding balance, with a brief reminder of how each one leads to a more balanced life. Also, turn to the Appendix on page 173 for some quick exercises and study questions that will help you get your arms and mind more firmly around each of these concepts.

1. Express gratitude.

Scripture has a different message than the world does when it comes to the idea of gratitude. From the Old Testament commands to give thanks for God's general and overall goodness, justice, and mercy to New Testament expressions of thankfulness to God for who He is and what He's already done with His overall plan, God wants gratitude to be part of your attitude.

Ephesians 5:19-20 says, "Sing and make music in your heart to the Lord, always giving thanks to God the Father for everything, in the name of our Lord Jesus Christ." *Always* and *everything* are key words; you don't get time off

Heartbeat Thankfulness

Our gratitude to God should be as regular as our beating heart.

—Anonymous

and you don't get to exclude anything. God has put or allowed everything that you experience into your life for a reason, and you're to be thankful for it and God's care for you.

The Bible tells us to give thanks for everything—the good, the bad, and the ugly! Philippians 4:6-7 may be the best-known verse in the Bible when it comes to expressing your gratitude on your journey toward finding balance in life: "Do not be anxious about anything, but in everything, by prayer and petition, with thanksgiving, present your requests to God. And the peace of God, which transcends all understanding, will guard your hearts and your minds in Christ Jesus."

2. Be content.

Scripture defines contentment as denying yourself so that God can instill a sense of balance within you. This is an internal peace that is available if you surrender yourself to God and His will for your life. In John 14:27, Jesus said, "Peace I leave with you; my peace I give you. I do not give to you as the world gives. Do not let your hearts be

> ### Put Together
>
> May God, who puts all things together, makes all things whole,
> Who made a lasting mark through the sacrifice of Jesus, the sacrifice of blood that sealed the eternal covenant,
> Who let Jesus, our Great Shepherd, up and alive from the dead,
> Now put you together, provide you with everything you need to please him,
> Make us into what gives him most pleasure, by means of the sacrifice of Jesus, the Messiah.
> All glory to Jesus forever and always!
> Oh, yes, yes, yes.
> —Hebrews 13:20-21, MSG

troubled and do not be afraid." When Jesus commands you not to be troubled or afraid, He's talking about surrendering your cares and worries to God.

Contentment doesn't happen when you try to organize all of the things stacked up and backed up in your life. Instead of neatly stacking your worries and anxieties as high as you can figuratively reach, contentment involves limiting the number of concerns that you're trying to stack up. Contentment is about taking the stresses and pressures and illogical responsibilities that make you feel out of balance and surrendering those to God so that you can know His peace.

3. Serve others.

Serving others is interrelated with serving God. You can't truly serve others apart from serving God. If you try, it's just volunteering, not service. When you truly serve God, it means telling or demonstrating through your actions of God's plan to save mankind from sin and death.

First Corinthians 15:58 states, "Therefore, my dear brothers, stand firm. Let nothing move you. Always give yourselves fully to the work of the Lord, because you know that your labor in the Lord is not in vain." When Paul mentioned "the work of the Lord" in this passage, he was talking about the work and labor of letting others know about His plan to redeem the world.

Ephesians 6:7-8 echoes this intertwining nature of your service to God and others: "Serve wholeheartedly, as if you were serving the Lord, not men, because you know that the Lord will reward everyone for whatever good he does."

The act of serving others will only feel empty if you do it for your own gain or reward. Why would you want to do that anyway? Certainly, you can't gain any merit or worthiness with God. It is only when you have the attitude that you're serving God because it's a privilege He's given you—the joy of being a part of furthering His plan for redeeming people—that we receive the reward God promises as a wonderful by-product.

4. Endure suffering.

God does have a purpose for allowing you to go through trials and hardships. Through Scripture, God reveals so much about His relationship with you, including why you'll endure suffering in your faith journey with Him.

- He promises that you won't go through more than you can handle. (Psalm 34:17-18)
- Your suffering is an honor—it identifies you with Christ. (Philippians 1:29)
- With suffering comes the power of resurrection and triumph over death. (Philippians 3:10)
- Suffering proves that God loves you as His very own child. (Hebrews 12:7)

- Suffering makes you holy. (Hebrews 12:10)
- Suffering develops perseverance. (James 1:2-3)
- Suffering helps you learn to respond without retaliation. (1 Peter 2:23)

Once you grasp that God allows your suffering to transform you into a more Christlike person, then you can learn how balance comes through trials and hardships.

- God's plans and purpose for you are worked out in great detail, including your suffering. (Jeremiah 29:11)
- The refining process of suffering makes your service to God useful for carrying out His big-picture plan. (2 Timothy 2:20-21)
- In light of eternity, your suffering is light and momentary. (2 Corinthians 4:16-17)

One of God's greatest desires for you is that you develop Christlike character. When godly character saturates your very being and even begins to radiate from you, then you've grasped what it means to have balance in your life. Ephesians 4:14-15 provides a word picture of what happens in this process: "Then we will no longer be infants, tossed back and forth by the waves, and blown here and there by every wind of teaching and by the cunning and craftiness of men in their deceitful scheming. Instead, speaking the truth in love, we will in all things *grow up* into him who is the Head, that is, Christ" (emphasis added).

Other Voices

I'm not a fan of pain. I don't know why I need it in order to live out God's purpose for me. But I do know that God knows. And if I trust Him to work it all out for good, He always does. God must balance my life for me—not me—and I have to trust the way He chooses to do it.

—Lisa

5. Defeat sin.

Sin is anything that keeps you separated from God. What a dilemma—you can't have a relationship with God with sin in your life, yet it's the sin in your life that keeps you from having a relationship with God.

Scripture says you can work on ways to stop sinning, and God will give you the strength you need:

- Love God more than you love your sin. (Psalm 66:18)
- Live according to God's Word. (Psalm 119:9)
- God won't allow you to face more temptation than you can handle, and He will provide ways for you to resist temptations. (1 Corinthians 10:13)

Of course, God wants you to stop sinning. But because it's impossible to not sin, He offers His forgiveness—provided through Christ's death on the cross and His resurrection from the dead. The apostle Paul put it this way:

> ### A Shared Life of Light
>
> If we claim that we experience a shared life with him and continue to stumble around in the dark, we're obviously lying through our teeth—we're not *living* what we claim. But if we walk in the light, God himself being the light, we also experience a shared life with one another, as the sacrificed blood of Jesus, God's Son, purges all our sin.
>
> —1 John 1:6-7, MSG

"Therefore, there is now no condemnation for those who are in Christ Jesus, because through Christ Jesus the law of the Spirit of life set me free from the law of sin and death" (Romans 8:1-2).

You simply have to accept God's forgiveness, and He gladly removes sin and death from your life and begins a wonderful and indescribable personal relationship with you!

6. Stop negative behaviors.

Negative behaviors are just sins too. But their lure may be so strong or their pleasure so great that they become a wall between you and God. God is there, patiently waiting, knowing that He's already offered you His forgiveness and a relationship with Him if you'll simply accept it. But guilt, pleasure, pride, feelings of unworthiness, or whatever stop you from saying, "I'm sorry, God, please forgive me. I want to be close to You as You've promised so that I can live for You."

Choosing these behaviors is like settling for second best. Whether they bring pleasure or provide an escape from your troubles, they're not as good as *the best*—a personal and fulfilling relationship with God. Jesus said, "No one can serve two masters. Either he will hate the one and love the other, or he will be devoted to the one and despise the other" (Matthew 6:24). In other words, anything you choose over God—including addictions and negative habits and behaviors—is what you become a slave to.

The lure of negative behaviors may be so strong or their pleasure so great that they become a wall between you and God.

However, Paul said that by choosing to follow Christ, obeying Him, and relying on His strength, you can be set free from this bondage. He wrote, "Thanks be to God that, though you used to be slaves to sin, you wholeheartedly obeyed the form of teaching to which you were entrusted. You have been set free from sin and have become slaves to righteousness" (Romans 6:17-18).

God wants you to have His best: "This is my prayer: that your love may abound more and more in knowledge and depth of insight, so that you may be able to discern what is best and may be pure and blameless until the day of Christ, filled with the fruit of righteousness that comes through Jesus Christ" (Philippians 1:9-11).

7. Deepen relationships.

The Bible has a lot to say about how Christians should conduct themselves in relationships. So this book can only serve as a primer. This list of general principles, based on the "one anothers" of the New Testament, should bring balance to your relationships and your life.

- "Love one another" (John 13:34). Imagine what your relationships would look like if you loved the people around you in the unconditional, unselfish, and sacrificial way that Jesus demonstrated love during His earthly life and ministry.

- "Honor one another above yourselves" (Romans 12:10). The big idea here is for you to treat people—in your words and actions—as Christ would treat them.

- "Be at peace with each other" (Mark 9:50). Even if you're the most intro-verted person around, your authentic and peaceful relationships will attract people who'll see that you're a good friend.

> ### Forget Yourself
>
> Develop interest in life as you see it; in people, things, liter-ature, music—the world is so rich, simply throbbing with rich treasures, beautiful souls, and interesting people. Forget yourself.
>
> —Henry Miller

- "Accept one another" (Romans 15:7). Think about who you were before you became a Christian—were you living a life worthy of Christ's love? Accept people as they are—don't try to change them. Transforming them is God's job, not yours (Romans 12:2).

- "Teach and admonish one another" (Colossians 3:16). Take in God's Word to the extent that you can interact wisely in your relationships.

- "Serve one another" (Galatians 5:13; 1 Peter 4:10). God doesn't give you spiritual gifts to be used selfishly. He expects you to use your gifts to minis-ter to others.

- "Carry each other's burdens" (Galatians 6:2). If you're a follower of Christ, you'll care so much for the people around you that you'll walk alongside them when they're struggling with any sort of superior attitude.

- Be patient with one another (Ephesians 4:2). Patience means not giving up on your friends and family. This includes practicing unconditional love when someone wrongs you.

- "Encourage one another and build each other up" (1 Thessalonians 5:11). Remind your friends and family how much they mean to you, how much you care for them, and how you appreciate having a relationship with them.

8. Practice accountability.

Accountability is evidenced by your integrity, which is demonstrated by the way you act or speak (Matthew 12:33-37). What you do and say reveal what's in your heart. You might be able to fake it for a while, but eventually what's in your heart will come out in your words and actions. Accountability means no longer trying to fake it, allowing another person or a group of people to know you well enough to call you on it when you do. Balance comes because you stop wasting time and energy trying to be something you're not.

Of course, this transformation is impossible without a relationship with Christ. Romans 12:2 says, "Do not conform any longer to the pattern of this world, but be transformed by the renewing of your mind." Only Christ can carry out the process of transforming you and your heart, though He may use people you're accountable to—an individual or group you ask to hold you accountable, as well your spouse, employer, coworkers, clients, church, small group, and so on.

9. Celebrate victories.

Celebrating life's "wins" and appropriately noting its "losses" can bring balance to your life. At first, it might seem awkward to focus on celebrating the little victories—and even the defeats—of your life. But once you get the hang of making those events more memorable, you'll find that you feel a lot more content about life. It's like taking gratefulness to the next level and saying, "I'm so thankful for this that I'm going to commemorate it and remember it."

You can celebrate both big events and smaller ones. You can also commemorate in some way the less enjoyable times of your life—such as losing a job, a divorce, a child going off to college, a foreclosure of property or bankruptcy, a change in living conditions, a change in work hours or conditions—any event you think God is using to teach you.

> ### Two Sides of a Coin
>
> Celebration can really come about only where fear and love, joy and sorrow, tears and smiles can exist together.
> —Henri Nouwen

10. Set priorities.

In addition to the many spiritual imperatives you can follow to find balance, you can also do practical things. Setting priorities is one place to start.

Prioritizing can help bring balance to your life by helping you analyze if a task or responsibility needs to be accomplished immediately or if it can wait. Does a task need to be broken down into a number of steps or can you accomplish it all at once?

Most of the things you need to get done have some level of urgency and some level of importance. You'll naturally find yourself working on the urgent things first. But make time to focus on important tasks before they become urgent. A sense of balance comes by having some control over this tangled web—having a plan of attack for getting things done.

There are a lot of ways to prioritize the tasks and routines of your life. You can divide them into areas of life: work, home, church, family, and so on. Or you can think of how you spend a typical day and list your tasks on daily planner pages to create some habits and routine.

But be careful about what you prioritize. Setting priorities works well for tasks because they're usually quantifiable. But the same strategy might not work in relationships because your goal there is to improve quality, not just to "get things done."

Appendix

Personal Exercises

These exercises and study questions are based on the top ten list in **Living Out Balance Every Day** starting on page 163. They'll help you examine how you're doing in each area and help you bring more balance into your life in practical ways.

You'll find space to write your answers below each question, or you can use another sheet of paper. You might want to repeat these exercises every two or three months, or complete one per week on a rotating cycle.

You decide—they're meant to help *you* find balance in *your* life.

1. Express gratitude.

Down the left side of this page, list as many things as you can think of that went wrong in the past week or two. Note both large and small disappointments, concerns, problems, and negative circumstances that you faced.

Now, next to each word, list a way that each negative situation might teach you something. More specifically, what do you think God is trying to teach you in each situation?

Finally, write down a way that you can express your gratitude to God for bringing each circumstance into your life. A few months from now, come back to this page and see if your guess about God's teaching was correct.

2. Be content.

Along the left side of this page, list the major circumstances that are adding stress to your life right now. What puts the most pressure on you—work, school, family relationships, marital problems, parenting pressures, unresolved issues from the past, worries about the future, finances, concerns about your security or safety? Don't limit yourself to these areas of worry. And if possible, try to be more specific. For example, instead of "finances," write, "I'm worried about how I'll pay the rent at the first of the month."

Now, look at your list. Next to each stress, write an S if you've surrendered that worry to God; write an O if you've kept ownership of it.

Look through your list again. Are there any areas of stress that you can eliminate from your life? List how you might get rid of those. For example, write, "I will ask my spouse to drive our kids to their weekly music lessons every other week."

Finally, ask God to give you the courage to surrender all of your concerns to Him. Return to this list in a week or two and cross off areas that you've eliminated. Change Os to Ss if you've surrendered additional areas to the Lord.

3. Serve others.

List on this page the ways that you serve others. Maybe you sing in the choir or on the worship team at your church. Perhaps you deliver meals to elderly people and those with disabilities. Or maybe you volunteer at your children's school.

Remember how serving relates to balance? Serving others will feel empty if you only do it for your own gain or reward. Be honest: Do you serve because you like to hear how wonderful you are because of the sacrifices you're making?

True service—and ultimately a sense of balance—will come when you're certain that your work is part of furthering God's plan for redeeming people.

Look at your list with these thoughts in mind. If you're just volunteering because it "makes you feel good," consider finding a new way of serving God and others, or at least think and pray about how you can change your perspective of what you're doing. How can you change any selfish acts of service into ones that glorify God and bring people into His kingdom?

4. Endure suffering.

Whenever suffering rears its ugly head in your life, you may not feel up to making lists or completing exercises. So find balance and comfort by reading and meditating on Psalm 34. If you can't even muster the energy to look it up, here are some of David's words (34:4-8,17-20) from *The Message* by Eugene Peterson:

When I was desperate, I called out,
and GOD got me out of a tight spot.

GOD's angel sets up a circle
of protection around us while we pray.

Open your mouth and taste, open your eyes and see—how good GOD is.
Blessed are you who run to him. . . .

Is anyone crying for help? GOD is listening,
ready to rescue you.

If your heart is broken, you'll find GOD right there;
if you're kicked in the gut, he'll help you catch your breath.

Disciples so often get into trouble;
still, GOD is there every time.

He's your bodyguard, shielding every bone;
not even a finger gets broken.

5. Defeat sin.

Study time! Read James 4. From verses 1-5, list some of the sins that the author identifies. Why do you think these characteristics and behaviors are sinful?

Now reread the rest of the chapter (verses 7-17). How does James say that you can overcome sin and negative behaviors in your life?

6. Stop negative behaviors.

Look at your list of sins from exercise 5. Can you identify any of these in your own life? Or are you struggling with a repeated sin that isn't on this list?

Review your list of ways to defeat sin. Ask God to give you His strength and power for defeating these sins. Thank Him that He forgives your sins. Be honest— tell Him that you know you can't stop committing the same sinful behaviors without His help; He knows your heart anyway. Thank Him that He's right there, patiently waiting for you to move back into His loving presence.

7. Deepen relationships.

List down the left side of this page the eight or ten most important relationships (aside from your relationship with God) that you have—your spouse, children, parents, friends, and so on. List each person by name.

Turn back to **Can I achieve balance in my relationships? Can other people help me find balance in life?** starting on page 100. Read through the list and descriptions of the "one anothers" from the New Testament.

Now, next to each person you listed, write one or two of the "one another" qualities that you could "do" to make the biggest difference in that person's life. For example, if you constantly battle with a strong-willed child, next to her name, write, "be patient with one another."

Then list one or two actions you can take—practical ways you can live out the quality you've listed. For example, with the strong-willed child, write, "When she speaks to me, I'll listen to the end of her sentences and repeat back what she's telling me. I'll give my best effort to listening to the things that most frustrate her."

Spend some time in prayer asking God to help you strengthen your most important relationships.

8. Practice accountability.

Read Ephesians 4:20-32. Paul writes here of ways that children of God can stay pure. List as many qualities of a pure life as you can.

If you regularly meet with another Christian who holds you accountable (an accountability partner), make notes of ways he or she can help hold you accountable for the different items on this list.

If you don't have an accountability partner, ask God to give you ideas of someone you could start meeting with. Make notes on the list regarding areas of your life where you need to be held accountable. And pray that even now God will help you work on these areas.

9. Celebrate victories (and commemorate defeats).

Making the events—good and bad, big and small—in your life memorable is like taking gratitude to the next level: "I'm thankful for what happens to me—so thankful that I'm going mark the occasion to help me remember it." And your attitude of gratitude to God can bring balance to your life.

List some things that you don't celebrate but could start: birthdays, anniversaries, job promotions, good grades, a new house, a new baby, graduations, a new job. Think about how celebrating the good things in life can give you a sense of balance. See page 115 for some simple ways you can rejoice over the little victories in life. Try to use one of these each week.

Now list some less enjoyable events that you wouldn't consciously think to commemorate, but could start: a financial failure, the breakup of a relationship, losing a job. Reflect on these questions: Why do you think it's important to remember these events? How can your failures teach you to succeed the next time you try something? How can you focus on what God is trying to teach you through these times? See pages 115-116 for some ways you can observe even the down times in your life.

10. Set priorities.

If you're teetering on the edge of burnout because of all the things you have to accomplish, use the chart on page 130 to organize all your tasks into a manageable battle plan.

A good reason to prioritize all the tasks in your life is to clear your head for bigger goals, dreams, and visions. For fun, think ahead five years. What would you like to accomplish during that timeframe, starting now. Make a list. Or imagine that you have to write a biography a few paragraphs long that lists your accomplishments during the past five years (again, put yourself five years from the present, and write your biography from now until that point in the future).

Evaluate what you've written. Did your dreams and visions include your family? Your work? What about God—did your goals and accomplishments include the things that God might have in store for you in the next five years?

Spend some time in prayer, asking God to set your sights higher for tomorrow by helping you clear your mind of the things that are weighing you down today. And ask God to give you goals that will glorify Him and give Him delight.

Notes

Introduction
1. "Is the American Dream Negotiable?" insert, *Adbusters* (January/February 2001), Vol. 9, No. 1, p. 14.

Defining Balance
1. *Encarta Reference Encyclopedia*, Encarta.msn.com, Entry: Hughes, Howard Robard.
2. Kenneth Barker, editor, The NIV Study Bible, New International Version (Grand Rapids, MI: Zondervan, 1985), p. 1604.
3. Neil Clark Warren, *Finding Contentment* (Nashville, TN: Thomas Nelson, 1997), subheads in chapter 8.
4. Carol Kent and Karen Lee-Thorp, *Basics of a Balanced Life* (Colorado Springs, CO: NavPress, 2000), p. 47.
5. Richard A. Swenson, M.D., *Margin* (Colorado Springs, CO: NavPress, 1992), p. 216.

What Does the Bible Say About Balance?

1. I heard a version of this—told far better than I'm able to retell it—on Paul Harvey's radio program "The Rest of the Story" while driving home from work one day. I searched for a transcript but couldn't find one.

2. Reuters Limited, AOL News: Gore's Concession Speech, 12-13-00.

3. Kirby Page, "Precious in God's Sight," *Hymns for the Family of God* (Nashville, TN: Paragon Associates, Inc., 1976), p. 673.

4. Richard J. Foster, *Celebration of Discipline* (San Francisco, CA: Harper & Row, 1978), p. 30.

5. This and all other Henri Nouwen quotations in this book are taken from *Seeds of Hope: A Henri Nouwen Reader*, Robert Durback, editor (New York: Image Books, 1997).

6. "In Need of a Prayer," Yankelovich Partners for Lutheran Brotherhood, reported in *USA Today*, (April 10, 1998), Life section, p. 1.

Why Do Things Seem Out of Balance?

1. Guinness World Records website, www.guinnessworldrecords.com, Category: Sports, Most basketballs dribbled simultaneously.

2. Kenneth Barker, editor, The NIV Study Bible, New International Version (Grand Rapids, MI: Zondervan, 1985), p. 1714.

3. H. L. Wilmington, editor, *The Book of Bible Lists* (Wheaton, IL: Tyndale, 1987), p. 315.

4. Facts gathered and summarized from 1000-2000 World History www.fact-monster.com, 2000 Learning Network.

Going After Balance

1. Adapted from a brief list I photocopied and taped inside the back cover of my study Bible many years ago; I looked for the original source but couldn't find one. My apologies to the original author(s).

2. Kevin Graham Ford, *Jesus for a New Generation* (Downers Grove, IL: InterVarsity, 1995), p. 29.

3. Donald S. Whitney, *Spiritual Disciplines for the Christian Life* (Colorado Springs, CO: NavPress, 1991), p. 17.

4. This section adapted from Donald S. Whitney, *Spiritual Disciplines for the Christian Life.* I couldn't hope to create a better summary of spiritual disciplines than in this great book by Don Whitney. The ten disciplines listed here are identified by him. I've added my reflections on how each discipline relates to balance in life. The description of each discipline is a brief summary of what he has written. All direct quotes are noted separately.

5. Whitney, pp. 65-66.

6. Whitney, p. 87.

7. Whitney, p. 116.

8. Whitney, p. 140.

9. Whitney, p. 184.

10. Whitney, p. 205.

11. Whitney, p. 224.

Seeking Balance in Your Own Life

1. Richard A. Swenson, M.D., *Margin* (Colorado Springs, CO: NavPress, 1992), p. 220.

2. Martin Camp, *Life on the High Wire: Faith and a Man's Search for Balance* (Nashville, TN: Dimensions for Living, 1997), p. 61.

3. Quoted by Pam Slater in "Workaholism No Longer Viewed As an Admirable Trait," at SiouxCityJournal.com.

4. Laura S. Struhl, Ph.D, "Avoiding Workaholism," *Self-Help Magazine,* May 26, 1998, www.shpm.com/articles/wf/work.html, copyright 1994-2001 by Pioneer Development Resources, Inc.

5. "Who's a Workaholic?" www.findarticles.com/m1121/9_249/61891317/p1/article.jhtml, copyright 2000, Penton Media, Inc.; Gale Group.

6. Struhl.

7. "Is the American Dream Negotiable?" insert, *Adbusters* (January/February 2001), Vol. 9, No. 1, p. 14.

8. E. C. McKenzie, editor, *14,000 Quips & Quotes* (Grand Rapids, MI: Baker, 1980), pp. 340-347.

9. Liz Curtis Higgs, *Only Angels Can Wing It* (Nashville, TN: Thomas Nelson Publishers, 1995), p. 6.

Author

Brad Lewis is a senior acquisitions editor at NavPress. He is also a contributing editor to *Rev.* magazine for pastors. He served as general editor for *The Pastor's Bible* (Zondervan/Group); five years as editor, then editorial director, of *Christian Parenting Today* magazine; and five years as assistant editor of *Decision* magazine at the Billy Graham Evangelistic Association. He earned a bachelor's degree in Communications-Journalism at Bethel College in St. Paul, Minnesota, and attended Wheaton College Graduate school in Wheaton, Illinois. Brad and his wife, Esther, live in Colorado Springs, Colorado, and are the parents of two sons, Nate and Trent.

LOADS OF INFORMATION IN A HANDY, COMPACT SIZE!

A Compact Guide to the Bible

Gain the maximum benefit from the Bible by understanding what you're reading, seeing the Scriptures' big picture, and learning to see your world from God's point of view.

A Compact Guide to the Bible (Karen Lee-Thorp) $9

A Compact Guide to the Christian Life

A Compact Guide to the Christian Life is an instant source of information on the Christian faith and how it applies to life in the modern world. Explore topics such as prayer, starting a small group, friendship, marriage, money, and much more!

A Compact Guide to the Christian Life (Karen Lee-Thorp) $9

A Compact Guide to Discovering God's Will

All of us face a major issue at some point in our lives, whether it be career selection, choice of college, or who to marry. Learn to listen to God and make choices that honor Him.

A Compact Guide to Discovering God's Will (Gordon S. Jackson) $9

Get your copies today at your local bookstore, visit our website at www.navpress.com, or call (800) 366-7788 and ask for offer **#6170** or a FREE catalog of NavPress products.

Prices subject to change.